TERRORISM: THREAT AND RESPONSE

Terrorism

Threat and Response

Eric Morris
and
Alan Hoe
with John Potter

MACMILLAN
PRESS

First published 1987

Published by
THE MACMILLAN PRESS LTD
Houndmills, Basingstoke, Hampshire RG21 2XS
and London
Companies and representatives
throughout the world

Typeset by Wessex Typesetters
(Division of The Eastern Press Ltd)
Frome, Somerset

Printed and bound in Great Britain at
The Camelot Press Ltd, Southampton

British Library Cataloguing in Publication Data
Morris, Eric
Terrorism: threat and response.
1. Terrorism
I. Title   II. Hoe, Alan
322.4′2   HV6431
ISBN 0–333–39887–4 (hardcover)
ISBN 0–333–39888–2 (paperback)

For Steve Cain, MBE

Contents

Part V   Protecting the Individual

Acknowledgements

Dr John Potter is a consultant psychologist and a specialist in the psychology of terrorism. We are particularly grateful for John's assistance and contribution to the book and in particular to Chapters 4 and 5 which reflect his experience.

Liz Cain undertook much of the initial research and the manuscript was typed by Pamela Morris. To Simon Winder at Macmillan for the production and to Keith Povey and his editorial team who improved the manuscript beyond measure our special thanks.

Finally, thank you to wives and families for their support and forebearance.

ERIC MORRIS
ALAN HOE

Introduction

The executive or casual traveller has never been more at risk from the actions of terrorists than he is today. The statistician could argue that this risk has been with us for the past three decades; this may well be so, but education and political and legal action resulting from 'lessons learned' appear to have had little effect in reducing the threat from the terrorist quarter; indeed, as this introduction is being written, the media reporters of the western world are vying desperately for the first place in gaining information on the fate of the passengers on a Pan-Am Boeing 747 taken over by Arab terrorists on a Karachi runway.

As the spinning of the web of international commerce and trade continues to encompass greater territory, so the business executive is forced into spending more time in travel on corporate affairs, travel which may take him to unfamiliar surroundings where he is subjected to strange laws and differing lifestyles; concomitantly, travel methods and facilities continue to improve and attract the casual passenger into making more adventurous journeys. Whilst security facilities and regulations may have improved at corporate headquarters, it is a sad fact that at travel termini, docks and airports there are still major flaws and weaknesses for the terrorist to exploit.

Continue to exploit these weaknesses he surely will, for what is more important to the terrorist than publicity and what gives more worldwide publicity than the hijacked aircraft, ship or train carrying a multinational passenger load which usually includes women and children?

Hijack is not the only risk. Apply the same travel situations to the increasingly frequent and indiscriminate use of explosives and the amount of publicity that such incidents gain for the bomber and the threat is heightened. In addition the last ten years have seen a steady, if still small, transference of the motive for kidnap from the purely criminal to being a relatively safe method of fund-raising by terrorist organisations. Who are the targets? They are certainly not restricted to the wealthy families; there is a growing recognition of the insurance policies carried by large corporations against this eventuality, thus placing the executive at risk at a very personal level.

Recalling some incidents from over a decade ago (this dating is deliberate); noting the inclusion of all forms of travel; and considering what international measures have or have not resulted from them; the internationally mobile executive would do well to ask himself: 'Are things better now? What should I know? What can I do?'

22 January 1961

On 22 January 1961, the Portuguese liner *Santa Maria* was seized, whilst at sea in the Caribbean, by a group of 70 men, led by Captain Henrique Galvao, a Portuguese political exile and a leading opponent of Dr Salazar's government. The liner was on a holiday cruise with over 600 multinational passengers on board including women and children.

At 01.30 hours, a group from amongst the passengers, armed with machine guns and hand grenades, took over the ship by assaulting the bridge, killing the third officer who resisted the assault, and injuring three other crew members.

Broadcasting a message to 'the newspapers of the world', Galvao stated that the '*Santa Maria* had been taken over in the name of the Independent Junta of Liberation of the Portuguese Republic led by General Humberto Delgardo the legally elected President who had been fraudulently deprived of his rights by the Salazar administration. . . .' Galvao went on to demand the support of all free governments and political recognition of *this* liberated part of the national territory.

An international search co-ordinated by the British frigate HMS *Rothesay* which was ordered to intercept and arrest, resulted in the *Santa Maria* being spotted by a US naval plane. Galvao was persuaded to alter course for Recife. On 31 January, Galvao had negotiations with a US naval admiral and on 1 February with a Brazilian admiral. These resulted in the *Santa Maria* entering Recife on 2 February, where most passengers and crew were allowed to disembark. On 3 February, Galvao accepted the Brazilian government's offer of asylum for himself and his followers.

This was the first modern hijack at sea. It lasted eleven days. One member of the crew was killed and three others were wounded. Galvao's declared aims were not met, although the 300 000 people who greeted the *Santa Maria* on her return to Lisbon will testify to the perverse curiosity of man and the effectiveness of the world publicity of the venture. Galvao and 32 others (including General Delgardo) were all tried *in absentia* in Lisbon. In a face-saving exercise they were sentenced to varying terms of long imprisonment; none of which were ever implemented.

The trial resulted in the Portuguese government issuing a decree making piracy (defined as the forcible seizure of a ship or aircraft) punishable by imprisonment of from 16 to 20 years.

This action by the Portuguese is one of the earliest attempts by modern government to stiffen its legislation as a means of eliminating terrorism.

On 10 November 1961, Captain Galvao again hit the headlines when his supporters seized a Portuguese airliner in mid-air, en route to Casablanca from Lisbon. They forced the pilot to circle over Lisbon while leaflets were dropped urging the population to help Galvao in the war against Salazar. The plane eventually landed in Tangier from where Galvao and his men were expelled. Again they were granted asylum in Brazil where they were forced to live under police surveillance. Captain Galvao can claim two 'firsts'; he highjacked a passenger liner at sea and hijacked an aircraft for a leaflet drop; moreover he is still a relatively free agent!

12 October 1967

On 12 October 1967, a BEA Comet was attacked and destroyed by a bomb whilst on a flight from Athens to Nicosia. It was widely reported that General Grivas (the EOKA terrorist who led the Greek Cypriot revolt against British rule) had intended to travel on that plane but had cancelled just before take-off and taken a later plane instead. Forensic examinations of the wreckage recovered from the sea proved that the bomb had been placed under a seat in the cabin. All 66 people on board were killed.

Did Grivas have prior intelligence? If so, why was this not used to save life? By what rules is the passage of such information between official and commercial agencies measured?

13 October 1977

On 13 October 1977, a Lufthansa Boeing 737 en route from Majorca to Frankfurt, was hijacked by a group calling themselves the 'Organisation of the Struggle against World Imperialism'. They were known to be working closely with the Red Army Faction. On board the aircraft were 87 German passengers and 5 crew. The terrorists demanded that the West German government release eleven Baader-Meinhof prisoners from their gaols and that the Turkish government simultaneously release two members of the Popular Front for the Liberation of Palestine. After the release, a sum of eight million pounds was to be handed over.

Over a period of 122 hours, the plane circled the Middle East, refuelling in Rome and Cyprus. Beirut, Kuwait and Damascus, along with various other Arab countries, refused landing permission and the aircraft eventually put down to refuel in Dubai. All negotiations with the hijackers went through the Defence Minister of the United Arab Emirates and just before the official deadline of noon on 16 October expired, the plane landed in Aden, against the will of the South Yemeni government. In Aden the runway was blocked off, forcing a landing on the soft sand alongside. Captain Schumann, the pilot, was shot after he insisted on getting out of the plane to inspect the undercarriage. With the co-pilot in command, the plane left Aden and on 18 October arrived at what was to be its final destination, Mogadishu in Somalia. At midnight the aircraft was successfully assaulted by the special unit of the West German Border Guards (GSG9). Two members of the British Special Air Service were present as advisers to the German group.

Two men and two women effected the hijack. Three of the terrorists were killed and the fourth was wounded and arrested. The leader, Zohair Youssef Akache, was later identified as having been responsible, in April 1977, for the murder of a former North Yemeni Prime Minister, his wife and another diplomat who was in his company at the time, in London.

Although the exact method is unknown, it is believed that the weapons were smuggled through the airport security system. This state of affairs still exists ten years later.

23 May 1977

On 23 May 1977, the first terrorist-co-ordinated 'double' incident took place in northern Holland. Both incidents happened simultaneously:

1. An inner-city train was seized whilst en route from Zwolle to Groningen. The driver escaped and raised the alarm leaving 52 hostages.

2. Thirty kilometres away from the hijacked train, a siege began at a school at Bovensmilde. There were 125 children and 5 teachers held hostage.

Both incidents were carried out by South Moluccan terrorists. They demanded the release of certain South Moluccan prisoners gaoled for other terrorist actions some two years earlier in Holland. They also demanded a Boeing 747 aircraft to fly them and a number of their hostages from Schipol to Benin where they hoped to find sanctuary.

The operations centre was set up within half a kilometre of the train in an underground bunker with a smaller command post close to the school in Bovensmilde. Both incident areas were cordoned off and a telephone link was established at the terrorists' request between the train and the school. On day three, a number of hostages were blindfolded and obliged to stand outside the train in full view and with ropes around their necks. At the school, fate took a hand and a virus infection forced the terrorists to release the schoolchildren; they retained all 5 teachers. Fourteen days of quite ineffectual negotiations followed during which time 3 hostages were released from the train: 2 pregnant women and a man who had suffered a heart attack.

At 05.00 hours the decision to use force was taken and members of the counter-terrorist forces, Royal Netherlands Marine Corps, Special Air Unit (BEE), were ordered to assault both the train and the school simultaneously. All hostages were safely released.

A relatively new tactic was openly brought into operation by the Dutch government in that a Crisis Centre was established in the Hague and a government psychologist constituted a decision-making part of the team.

9 March 1977

On 9 March 1977, three separate buildings in Washington DC, were seized by Muslim fanatics. For a period of 39 hours, they held 134 people hostage.

The Muslims were members of the Hanafi sect under the leadership of Khalifa Hamaas Abdul Khaalis. The Hanafi sect was a splinter group which had broken away from the organisation known as the Black Muslim. The breakup had occurred after the Black Muslim leader Malcolm X was assassinated.

To cause the maximum number of policing problems, the seizure of the three buildings was staggered. Firstly, at about 11.00 hours, the B'nai B'rith building belonging to a leading Jewish organisation was taken by 4 armed men with machetes and pistols. Somewhere between 10 and 100 people were held hostage. Following this, at midday, the National Islamic Centre in the Embassy district was secured by one gunman who held 15 people. Thirdly, about two and a half hours later, in the District of Colombia headquarters, the Washington City Hall building was under terrorist control. Prior to taking the building there was a gun battle in which a newspaper reporter was killed and a City Councillor was severely wounded in the head and chest. The Mayor and 4 others were taken hostage.

The City Police quickly contained all three sites and, using snipers, covered all exits. Shortly afterwards Khaalis made his demands known. He insisted on, and got, a telephone interview which was televised nationally on which he demanded that 6 prisoners, the murderers of 6 members of his family, be brought to him. (In 1973, Khaalis's home had been raided by 6 rival Muslims; his 5 children and 10-day-old grandson had been killed. The Hanafis had always blamed the Black Muslims for this outrage.) He further demanded that the film, 'Mohammed, Messenger of God', be banned from the television network in the USA (the portrayal of Mohammed the Prophet is considered high sacrilege in the Islamic faith). Lastly he asked for the sum of US$750 to be returned to him as his rightful property. (Some time earlier, Khaalis had been in court charged with contempt during the trial of members of the Black Muslim movement and the sum demanded was the amount of the fine he had been made to pay.)

The two latter demands were quickly met by the police in an attempt to persuade Khaalis into thinking that they were sympathetic in order that they could set up an effective telephone negotiation operation.

On 10 March, late in the day, the Ambassadors of Egypt, Pakistan and Iran all took their turn at negotiating with Khaalis. They were all allowed into the B'nai B'rith building where terrorist control was being co-ordinated, and eventually the terrorists allowed themselves to be persuaded into surrendering without further incident.

In late July 1977, all twelve Hanafi members were brought to trial. All were convicted of conspiracy and kidnapping, but in addition Khaalis and two of the men were also sentenced for the second degree murder of the newspaper reporter.

It is reliably reported that the City Police had made up their minds that the terrorists were not going to be allowed any form of safe conduct from the buildings.

September/October 1977

Doctor Hans Martin Schleyer was a leading industrialist and a prominent figure in West German society. President of the West German Employers Federation, government adviser on labour and economic problems and director of the giant Daimler-Benz industrial combine; his status was such that the police regarded him as a prime terrorist target and supplied him with four full-time bodyguards. Despite these precautions on 5 September 1977 Schleyer was ambushed in Braunfels. During the attack, machine-gun fire killed two police bodyguards, a security consultant and a driver; Schleyer himself was abducted.

Through the West German News Agency, the Hausner Commando Unit of the Red Army Faction claimed responsibility (Hausner, a Baader-Meinhof terrorist, had died of wounds during the raid on the German Embassy in Stockholm in 1976). A letter to the West German government laid out the terrorists demands. Each of the 14 Baader-Meinhof terrorists in Stuttgart prison was to be given £25 000 and released under safe-conduct to Frankfurt Airport. The prisoners were to be accompanied by M. Denis Payot, a Swiss lawyer and human rights campaigner, and Dr Martin Niemoller, a well-known anti-Nazi figure. The latter stipulation was presumably to guarantee the safe-conduct.

Proof that Schleyer was alive was passed in the form of a tape recording in which Schleyer gave the answers to personal questions posed to him by the police. On 9 September, Denis Payot agreed to serve as the channel of communication between the police and the terrorists. Various deadlines passed without incident and negotiations were conducted in an almost leisurely fashion. A 'final ultimatum' letter was passed to the Bonn office of the French News Agency, France-Presse, which contained a photograph of the still-alive Schleyer. Again, this deadline passed without incident.

Fate intervened in the first two weeks of October when three of the named Baader-Meinhof prisoners in Stammheim, Stuttgart, took their own lives and the strike force of GSG9 successfully assaulted the aircraft hijack at Mogadishu. This almost certainly sealed Schleyer's fate. His body was found in the boot of a car in Mulhouse,

Alsace, on 19 October 1977. The information showing where to locate him came as the result of a telephone call from the Red Army Faction to the left-wing Paris Newspaper, *Libération*. In what was obviously a revenge killing, Schleyer's throat had been cut. He had been held hostage for 43 days.

It is certain that Schleyer's death was pre-ordained when the West German government gave orders for the assault on the Lufthansa aircraft at Mogadishu and allowed press coverage of the Stammheim prisoners' suicides. It is interesting to note that there was no press conjecture on this at the time.

The reports related have covered virtually every form of transport used by the modern executive; each and every one of them involved innocent people being held hostage and in some cases killed. Likewise each incident produced a lesson for the authorities which was not necessarily learned. Even with the immense amount of modern international co-operation between police and intelligence agencies, the number of terrorist operations shows an inexorable increase. Consider the scale of incidents which have taken place at other venues in the last decade, where the traveller on business or pleasure has found himself from time to time, and the future seems bleak indeed.

Terrorist actions have occurred in hotels; in sports arenas; in restaurants; in the streets; in transport termini; in cinemas; in theatres; and in private homes. Where then does the traveller find peace and security? In short – he doesn't!

What the aware person can do, however, is to limit dramatically the risk on those occasions when he is under threat by fully understanding that threat. He can be educated into knowing the motivations, practices and methods of the modern terrorist. He can learn the simple rules of making himself a difficult target without necessarily destroying the quality of his own lifestyle.

It is not at all unusual for the wrong 'target' to be kidnapped by mistake, particularly in those countries where a cut-out system is used and the actual kidnappers are being hired for the 'snatch' rather than being the beneficiaries of the eventual ransom. Neither is it unusual for an executive to be abducted in order to bring pressure to bear on the owners of large wealthy corporations; and it is becoming increasingly frequent in Latin America for a person to be kidnapped simply because he 'looks like a man of substance'. There is something that the aware executive can do to reduce the personal risk in all these cases, and even if the worst happens and he is abducted or caught in a hijack, there are still disciplines he can observe which will be of great assistance to him during his possibly lengthy incarceration.

This book is designed to create an awareness in the modern travelling executive, but more than that, it is aimed at helping him to help himself in an unsympathetic world where terrorist actions can so often leave him at the mercy of untutored third-party actions.

Part I

The Nature and Extent of International Terrorism

1 Historical Perspectives

In recent years the free world has been witness to an ever-growing number of unorthodox political activists and movements, whose weaponry has ranged across the spectrum from civil disobedience to coup d'état; from tyrannicide to guerrilla war to terrorism. Such incidents have presented the press and media with a field day.

One result is that terrorism is seen by the public as something which is novel; and all too often this impression is given credence by commentators and policymakers alike. The truth is that political violence, often of the most unsavoury kind, has been with us throughout time. Today's terrorists take humans hostage. The Incas seized the idols of tribes they had conquered and held these hostage to ensure that the vanquished would not rebel. Beginning with Cain and Abel the Bible is littered with accounts of political violence, and it is the very heart of Greek and Roman history.

In their troubled province of Judaea, the Roman Army of occupation at the time of Jesus Christ had its hands full dealing with such trouble-makers as the Iscariots, and with the Sikarikin, the extreme wing of the Zionist Zealots. It was their rebellion that culminated in the tragedy of Massada, and which prompted the dispersion or diaspora of the Jews: the starting point for much of the conflict and bloody violence which is present in the Middle East today.

Brutus, portrayed by Shakespeare as a man of principle and high-minded beliefs, became a terrorist on the Ides of March, the day he helped assassinate Julius Caesar. Other such folk heroes of myth and legend were Robin Hood and William Tell who waged war on tyrants. Terrorism traces its origins back to the time honoured practice of tyrannicide.

The problem of whether tyrannicide can be condoned is a complex issue on both moral and political grounds. We cannot condemn such action out of hand, for clearly there have been times when there was no other redress against tyranny. In July 1944 Colonel Von Staufenberg failed in his attempt to kill Hitler. The 'General's Plot' was stillborn, and the Führer exacted a terrible revenge on the perpetrators, real and imaginary. There are those who to this day would maintain that it is 'not the job of the generals to "bump off"[1] political leaders'; an opinion no doubt shared by many in the West

German army of today. At the best this has to be an extremely narrow and naive view to take. Had the British Secret Service (or anybody else's for that matter) been so ordered in the later 1930s and had succeeded in 'bumping off' Adolf Hitler, it would have been an act of state-sponsored terrorism. It would also have been an act of liberation for a world otherwise condemned to the ravages of the Second World War.

'He has plundered our seas, ravaged our coasts, burnt our towns and destroyed the lives of our people.' Thus the authors of the American Declaration of Independence labelled King George III's use of terror as justification for what they clearly regarded as their own act of liberation. In such instances the killing of Redcoats and Loyalists became not murder, but an act of patriotism.

The difficulty is that throughout history every terrorist has claimed to be a liberator; battling against unspeakable despotisms and cruelties. The cynical view would be that such claims are validated on the single premise of success; in this instance measured by achieving victory over an oppressor and independence for the country. Every state is its own moral judge, the keeper of its own code of conduct and behaviour. In the world in which we live it could not be any other way. In the traumatic years of decolonisation following the Second World War there were many examples where 'yesterday's terrorist became today's freedom fighter and tomorrow's head of state'. Terrorism has an ancient lineage, but neither the law nor the so-called progress of mankind has done much to help clarify either its meaning or the acceptance of it.

Today the United States and Great Britain have taken a brave and defiant leading stand against modern terrorism, in particular singling out such countries as Libya and Iran for their coldblooded sponsorship of such acts. Yet the use of terror as an instrument of state craft has a venerable lineage.

Kidnapping can be traced back at least to the twelfth century when the English King, Richard the Lionheart, was held hostage in a Rhine castle until his subjects paid a 'king's ransom' to his captors, the Archduke of Austria and the Holy Roman Emperor. Later, children became a popular target for kidnapping and that is generally believed to be the origin of the term. In the seventeenth and eighteenth centuries infant children were kidnapped and sold into slave labour for the colonies in New England.

In the twelfth and thirteenth centuries, the cult of the Assassins did the bidding of their Ottoman overlords in the removal of opposition and dissent. Six hundred years later two of the more radical Jacobin leaders of the Committee of Public Safety in Paris, Robespierre and Louis St Just, inaugurated a reign of terror which reputedly claimed more than 40 000 lives. It began in September 1793, when the Revolutionary Convention, having guillotined King Louis XVI declared 'terror the order of the day', so as to eliminate all suspected enemies of the Republic. Beyond the borders of France, the crowned heads of Europe, stunned by the execution of the King, declared war on a revolution which they rightly saw as a challenge to their order in the world.

In more modern times, the Armenians in nineteenth-century Turkey rediscovered the efficacy of taking hostages, while the concept of systematic political terrorism first appeared at about the same time in the secret societies of Italy and Spain. By the middle of the century it had spread to the Germans, before the Russians took up the mantle.

The Russian terrorists were different, however, for they not only advocated an elaborate system of terrorism, they practised it as well. Anarchists and Revolutionaries made ready use of the letter bomb and the improvised explosive device (IED) and no capital in Europe was safe from their attacks. In Britain the area between Parliament and the square mile of the City of London witnessed a number of bombing incidents. In Paris, Berlin, Vienna and St Petersburg, notables were gunned down, victims of Anarchists, Nihilists and Revolutionary Terrorists who succeeded in making life at the turn of the century distinctly uncomfortable for those in public life. It is a historical fallacy to look upon the Japanese Red Army, Black September or the actions of Islamic Jihad as anything new.

The use of terror as a political instrument was a key element in Lenin's strategy for building the first communist state. At his direction, the Vecheka under Comrade Dzerzhinsky systematically terrorised the Russian populace. This set the precedent for even more repressive mechanisms under Stalin and his successors. Such mechanisms of terror as the OGPU became Stalin's vehicle for forcefully imposing his policy of Russification upon the Soviet Union. Its notorious successor, the NKVD, spearheaded the purges and demonstrated the long arm of state terror in 1940 with the assassination of the dissident Trotsky in Mexico. The NKGB was used to ensure that the conflict with Nazi Germany was indeed a 'Great Patriotic War' for Soviet citizens. The present-day KGB and the military GRU provide instructors for terrorist training camps in

Prague, Baku, Odessa and Tashkent. Their students come from many countries, thereby maintaining the historical continuity of Lenin's dictum to the effect that the Communist Party was based upon a principle of coercion which did not recognise any limitations or inhibitions. There can be little doubt that the tactics, techniques, philosophy and inspiration for the use of terrorism in the world today which are so well documented, came from the Soviet model which in turn has been carefully and systematically constructed.

Modern communications, in terms both of the media and of international travel, lend their support to the spread of terrorism. Other states, too, have for their own ends encouraged terrorism by providing money, support and sanctuary, abusing the privileges of diplomatic protocol in the process. For some, Cuba, North Korea, South Yemen and Libya, too it gives their leaders a certain feeling of power which they otherwise would not have in our status conscious world. It allows the more tyrannical to liquidate opponents living in exile, and to cause embarrassment to their foes. For these states such acts of terror are indeed a substitute for war.

Historical continuity is present in the technology of terrorism. Throughout time, whether it was the anti-Tsarist terrorists in the nineteenth century, the IRA's bid for independence after the Great War or in incidents today, terrorists have had the capacity for acquiring and using the latest technology. Guy Fawkes's attempt to blow up the English Parliament in 1604 with 36 barrels of gunpowder was a perfect case in point. There are times, too, when the technology deployed by the terrorist has caught authorities unawares. Islamic Jihad hit the US Marine compound in Beirut with an old truck crammed with explosives. The Marines were prepared for the car bomb, but their colonel had not thought to counter the threat posed by a truck load of explosives driven by a suicide bomber and 241 of his command were killed.

Terrorists are perfectly capable of exploiting whatever technology is to hand. They have moved quickly into the field of electronics in order to make bigger and better bombs. The terrorist bomber has been described as 'the poor man's airforce'. This may well be the case, but in incidents such as that in Beirut and others the terrorist is far more discriminating and accurate when it comes to the destruction of his target than the professional airforces have shown themselves to be in recent years.

Terrorism is a form of blackmail. It is a dirty business which can flourish in free societies because it requires the permissiveness of such societies in which to function. And when the security forces retaliate, the terrorist cries 'foul' and this preys on a democracy's sense of fair play. But terroristic blackmail is nothing new. Rudyard Kipling in his poem 'Danegeld' cites an example from Saxon times: 'If once you've paid him the Danegeld, you'll never get rid of the Dane.'

A new terrorism emerged in the immediate aftermath of the Second World War, which particularly in the Far East had exposed for all time the fallacy of a white machine-age supremacy, and thereby heralded the dawn of new nationalisms. Amongst the weakened discredited Imperial powers, there were some who recognised it was time to leave, for their days of power were over. Others simply created even more problems for themselves, as they sought to respond to irregular warfare and terrorism by the conventional tactics of 'fire and movement'.

Britain, having suffered the ravages of a terrorist guerrilla war in Ireland, now experienced something similar at the hands of the Jewish resistance movement, and their largely uncontrollable terrorists in Palestine. Little did the new Israelites appreciate that those others whom they displaced, the Palestinians, were to learn the bitter lessons well, and apply them when their time came.

The French army in Indochina failed to learn quickly enough that the 'People's Wars' of Mao Tse-Tung, Ho Chi Minh and Vo Hgugen Giap were multidimensional. The Americans for their part, brashly confident of their technological prowess, and 'scientific approach' to war, never came to terms with the defined objectives of North Vietnamese and Vietcong terrorist tactics until their involvement assumed the proportion of a national humiliation. The goal of the terrorist who operates in an anticolonialist context is the control of the populace, and thus the response which comprises military hardware conventionally deployed is largely irrelevant.

Yet Western armies think conventionally. Their officers are taught to think in terms of armies on the battlefield. Staff Colleges in Britain and the United States emphasise the European land battle and the tactical nuclear scenarios. Little enough time is spared to study the 'dirty little wars', and this despite the fact that since 1945 there have been only two years when the British army was at peace.

For a generation after the Second World War 'the dirty little wars' absorbed the attentions of the Western Powers to a greater or lesser extent, until they too became embroiled in a new violence. For these 'post industrial societies', as the sociologists were pleased to label them, terrorist groups emerged from the radical leftist student movements protesting at the materialism of countries who were in alliance with the United States. In 1968 campus unrest reached its peak. In April of that year Andreas Baader was caught in the act of setting fire to a department store in Frankfurt. His defence in court was that the fire was necessary to 'activate the masses'. Condemned to a prison term he had served but a short time before being freed by a group of supporters who included Ulrike Meinhof. So the Baader-Meinhof gang hit the headlines, chic terrorists who waged war on the Federal Republic from their BMW limousines.

Baader-Meinhof were a latter day Bonnie and Clyde, whose group formed the hard core of the Red Army Faction, a broad-based terrorist movement that drew its support from middle-class dropouts. They had their equivalents on both poles of the political spectrum in Italy; the Red Brigades were the best known. None of these groups could have functioned without a fairly extensive network of sympathisers. Professors, journalists and others of the intelligentsia ensured that the universities provided the spawning ground for the new terrorists; and for a time they were remarkably successful.

Even while the security forces tried to cope, terrorism from the Middle East spilled over into Europe. The Arabs had tried and failed in four conventional wars to defeat the Israelis, so the Palestinians resorted to a terrorist campaign aimed at Israeli people and property overseas, and those seen to be supporters of Israel.

In 1970 the Popular Front for the Liberation of Palestine inaugurated the thunderous era of Palestinian terrorism, hijacking and exploding airliners in Egypt and Jordan. Then in September 1972 the world was horrified to watch the shoot-out at Furstenfeldbrück Airport at Munich. Television cameras filmed as hostages from the Israeli Olympic Team, a police officer, a helicopter pilot and four of the captors were gunned down, in a police operation that went terribly wrong.

The Munich attack hit home that there was a new breed of terrorism loose. Munich was not a nationalist operation. It was a Palestinian operation in which members of Baader-Meinhof were involved in what the media claimed to be the new international terrorism.

Are the terrorists of today different from those in history? Certainly in one respect there is an immediate and stark departure. The terrorists of the past were desperately poor, whereas today it is big business. Movements like the Palestine Liberation Organisation have revenues greater than the Gross National Product of many states. Having so much money at their disposal, the PLO and its different factions took a lesson from organised crime. Following the precedents set by the Mafia in the United States and Italy, they made large investments of funds throughout Europe, entering the property market and speculating on the Stock Exchanges, thereby making even more money.

Another important source of revenue is drugs. At such international points of entry into Western Europe as Frankfurt, Charles de Gaulle and Heathrow, Palestinian groups provide couriers and smuggle in vast amounts of drugs in what has become a losing battle, to keep up with demand. Other terrorist groups are similarly involved. The IRA and Protestant paramilitary groups in Northern Ireland have invested heavily in the local economy, in property, labour and transport markets. In Latin America urban guerrilla groups of the 1960s had vast resources, while in Italy kidnapping and extortion yielded an estimated US$65 million in ransom payments by the middle 1970s. Money and means, transport and communications allow the modern terrorist to hit targets which previously were out of reach.

There is more terrorism now than in the past. In the period since the Yom Kippur War in 1973 there has been a tenfold increase in terrorist incidents. The targets have been Britain and West Germany, France and Italy, Israel and Japan, and above all the United States, whose citizens account for 30 per cent of terrorist victims.

There are those who see in this trend a conspiracy of professional terrorism which seeks to demoralize and subvert democratic societies. Such thoughtful commentators as Paul Johnson have noted that 'step by step, almost imperceptibly, without anyone being aware that a fatal watershed has been crossed, mankind has descended into an age of terror'.[2]

It is not the statistics of international terrorism which account for such widespread attention. In the worse period of US domestic turmoil, between 1965 and 1968, there were 214 people killed and 9000 injured as a result of student protest, political terrorism and ghetto riots. These figures can be compared to the 12 000 murders and 250 000 aggravated assaults which occur annually in the United States. Indeed there are more murdered annually in domestic strife or killed in automobile accidents in the States than die as a result of terrorist incidents worldwide.

So if statistically there does not seem to be a major problem, why the public concern? There are perhaps two reasons which help to explain public preoccupation with terrorism. The first is that terrorists resort to 'violence for effect'. The break with history lies in terrorists making propaganda by the deed. They choose to stage spectacular and violent displays. Kidnappings are internationally organised, reaching out across continents. Assassinations of the important, and random slaying of the innocent, capture the headlines or are set for prime-time coverage, seen in living rooms, on breakfast TV, in colour. The kaleidoscope of violence is beamed by satellite across the world and seen by millions.

Publicity underlines the desire of these men of violence for the magnification of their deeds, measured in column inches and airtime. Thus the target for the terrorist is the mass audience, who are angered, shocked and outraged by the crime. Similarly exposed are the national leaders whose performance is catalogued and scrutinised by the media. This too can so often work in favour of the terrorist. President Carter agonised publicly for 444 days when American diplomats were held hostage in Tehran, and then organised a rescue mission which ended in fiasco and humiliation.

Over time of course, the public becomes immune to the cacophony of violence. The death of a soldier in Northern Ireland or a sectarian killing no longer capture media attention to the degree they would have in the past. This in part explains the second and most frightening aspect of contemporary terrorism and public concern. It is the sheer randomness of the violence which causes such alarm.

In Britain the people were stunned by the attack launched by the IRA on the Grand Hotel in Brighton. Terrorists came within an ace of slaughtering the Prime Minister and her Cabinet. Even more chilling was the communique which followed: 'The myth that the British Government is impregnable has been blown – and that alone increases our daring and confidence. There will be future attacks – there will always be attacks in Britain – we will pick the time and place carefully. But we are hardly going to give notice.'[3]

Relatively small groups possess an ability to destroy, to cause trouble and strife to the rest of us which is out of all proportion to their actual strength. Herein lies the threat of the modern terrorist, from which none of us are immune.

NOTES

1. Montgomery of Alamein, *History of Warfare* (London: Rainbird, 1968), p. 525.
2. Paul Johnson, quoted in David Fromkin's 'The Strategy of Terrorism' (*Foreign Affairs*, July 1975).
3. Spokesman of the IRA quoted in an interview with the Sinn Fein Journal *An Poblacht*, August 1985.

2 Terrorism

What is terrorism? There seems to be little agreement among the experts when it comes to definitions. We can quibble over definitions as to what precisely does or does not comprise an act of terrorism, but such semantics dissolve when a disguised bomb (known in the highly specialised world of bomb disposal as an Improvised Explosive Device or IED) explodes with devastating effect in a department store packed with Christmas shoppers; or when an airliner disintegrates in flight.

The term nowadays is a pejorative, it is the label used by the threatened. In the nineteenth century a terrorist was someone who engaged in a special kind of violence against the state. The term had a conventional, and convenient, revolutionary usage, acknowledged as such by both perpetrators and their victims on targets. This no longer seems to be the case today – the former are guerrillas, freedom fighters, fedayeen, but never terrorists. The latter for their part use terrorism to describe any act which involves an attack on the general functioning of society. It embraces a spectrum of violence from skyjacking through indiscriminate bombing to politically motivated kidnappings, assassinations, ritualistic murder and the material destruction of property.

It is not possible to construct a single theory or definition which can encompass so wide a spectrum, and it is wrong to allow such an indiscriminate tally of evil to reside under the heading of terrorism. The vagueness with which the term is used is a major source of misunderstanding of the nature of, and thus the threat posed by, the terrorist.

Rebellions, street battles, civil and industrial strife, insurrection, rural guerrilla warfare, coups d'état, animal rights and environmentalist pressure groups have all been at various times described as terrorist. The term slips and slides with elusive imprecision which is fine for the gurus of the media but leads us into all sorts of difficulties. It inflates the statistics and thus makes the problem appear to be even bigger than it really is, thereby causing even greater alarm. Indiscriminate labelling also complicates the task of understanding the character of terrorism, and until we understand the problem then we are not going to cope with it.

Writers and academics when confronted with this issue adopt

different approaches. One school maintains that the key to the solution of understanding terrorism lies in understanding people. This method, much favoured by psychologists, emphasises a study of 'who' are the terrorists, and it does have obvious limitations. No such expert can talk to, let alone psychoanalyse the behaviour of, a real live terrorist. Active members are too elusive for prolonged or in-depth analysis. Those who have been captured or interned could possibly reveal information which is of use, but because they are no longer in a 'live state', its value is limited. Finally those who have retired or 'reformed', like veterans everywhere, are inclined to adjust memory, and in this case to the present cause. It does seem to be dangerously misleading to generalise about men and women on the run, people without names who live a lie, a life which is covert and secretive.

Drawing general conclusions about selected terrorists where comparisons of behaviour cross cultural boundaries is to be avoided. The Irish, Germans, Black Americans and Arabs all perform similar acts of violence, but does this mean they have personality traits and other human characteristics in common? They may have youth, commitment and dedication in common; but fighter pilots and professional boxers share the same qualities. Can there be much value in seeking links or areas of common ground between a Protestant Belfast ship worker, a Palestinian graduate of the American University of Beirut, a Black Militant in a New York ghetto, a Spanish Army Colonel or a Latin American priest?

On 30 May 1972 three members of the Japanese Red Army disembarked from a scheduled flight at Lod Airport in Israel. Once inside the Terminal buildings, they reached into their hand baggage, pulled out machine pistols and grenades, and opened fire. In a kamikaze style massacre they slaughtered all round them until they were gunned down. Twenty-four people were killed and a further seventy injured. The majority of the victims were not Israelis, but were from a party of Puerto Rican Christians on a pilgrimage to the Holy Land.

One of the three terrorists survived, and under interrogation revealed the tangle web of international terrorism. The group were recruited, and then taken to North Korea where they were trained; they were supported by funds from West Germany. Flown to the Middle East, the three received final training in guerrilla camps first in Syria and then in the Lebanon. In Italy they were briefed and armed by their client, in this instance the Popular Front for the Liberation of Palestine (PFLP), before catching a flight on what was intended to be a one-way mission to Israel.

When asked why he had become a terrorist mercenary, the survivor, who was a boy of 15, admitted that he had joined the Japanese Red Army because his elder brother was a member. How can the forces of law and order take account of sibling behaviour?

Psychologists have contributed some useful information on the pathological end of the terrorist spectrum. Many acts of violence, especially when one looks at the long list of American assassinations, have been committed by those who have been seriously mentally disturbed. The assassins' minds, and thus their motives for action are an incoherent mix of fantasy, perceived injustice and half-baked political aspirations.

There are notable exceptions, but most aircraft hijackers can be explained in psychotic terms rather than as holding a coherent political grievance seeking expression through deeds and actions. There are, too, the psychotic terrorists, the mentally disturbed such as psychopaths, attracted by the aura of violence into terrorist groups. Others find their way into police and paramilitary forces worldwide. Professor Richard Clutterbuck, one of the most eminent British authorities on terrorism maintains that terrorists attract the mad. They also make the sane mad through deliberate acts of initiation such as killings. Psychology has also advanced some useful techniques and tactics in the highly charged field of hostage bargaining, but it would appear there is still much to be done before we can make valid comments about the mind of the assassin or the personality profile of the sane bomber.

Emotions can too often get in the way when trying to understand terrorism. Whichever approach is adopted, it is vital to remain objective. Some adopt the stance that all terrorists are warped, their politics too extreme to be taken seriously, their demands so unrealistic that it is impossible to reach an accommodation or compromise through negotiation.

In August 1985 radical Shi-ite terrorists shot to death an American serviceman on a TWA flight, and then proceeded to shuttle desperately between Algiers and Beirut. There seemed to be no way out in this classical type of terrorist incident. The hardliners failed to convince the authorities that the answer lay in shooting out the plane's tyres while on the runway in Algiers. Thereafter they were convinced there was no hope of compromise, and that all attempts at diplomacy were a waste of time. President Reagan and his advisers, despite the rhetoric of public postures, quickly came to appreciate that terrorism is not a clear-cut issue. The Administration proceeded to negotiate in a series of sensitive and delicately balanced diplomatic manoeuvres. The price the United States had to pay in the process was to give the terrorists status and legitimacy as world actors, and for some critics that, as a matter of principle, was too high a price.

The Beirut hijack was an incident full of paradox. Secretary of State Shultz sought the assistance of Syria in securing the release of the aircraft, its crew and passengers. At the same time he did not depart from his Department's public stance that Syria was firmly lodged in the camp of those states that sponsor terrorism alongside South Yemen, Libya and Iran. The emergence of President Assad and the leadership of the Amal Militia as honest brokers to the settlement was a contradiction to US foreign policy which caused even greater confusion in such an emotionally charged incident. Nevertheless when this is set against the release of the hostages, it seems a small price to pay.

The TWA hijack in Beirut shows that expert opinion in the free world is no nearer to understanding terrorism and who terrorists are. All that we can do is examine the bounds or limits to terrorism and try to plot a sensible course through the confusions and contradictions.

The first limit must lie in the violence of the act. Terrorism is the threat or use of extraordinary violence for political ends. Such acts of terrorism, however, are symbolic rather than instrumental, and are undertaken for psychological rather than material effect. The late Raymond Aron, a French commentator and expert political scientist defined it in the following way: 'An act of violence is labelled "terrorist" when the psychological effects are out of all proportion to its purely physical result.'[1] It is this feature of the psychological input which is the keynote to understanding terrorism today. The armed propaganda of violence is a 'theatre' for the terrorist where the target is the audience reached by way of the media. In this context the victim of the terrorist act simply becomes a symbol.

The quintessence of terrorism centres on three factors, the source of violence, the audience and the victim. It is as well to remember that the necessary concomitant of terrorism is fear, and the ultimate objective is coercion.

Terrorists have become very skilled in their use of violence to attract attention. In many instances the interim objective is to propel their movement not towards an assumption of power, but only to prominence. Thus a spectacular assassination, or a televised negotiation over the fate of hostages, can sustain the organisation, help spread the message and thereby attract sympathy and even recruits to the cause.

Terrorism is practically worldwide, so we need to take into consideration the society in which it occurs. In some parts of the world there are societies in which violence is already endemic. Here violence becomes habitual, it is the custom of the tribe, so ritualistic that many acts which might otherwise draw attention, go unnoticed. Other societies are ruled by regimes where repression, torture and judicial assassination become the norm of government, and the people are terrorised. Those in opposition have to resort to the tactics of the regime, seeking out and slaying their opponents.

In more recent times another sort of terror emerges, particularly in those countries where government has shown itself unable to contain a violent opposition or challenge. The vigilantes of order take the law into their own hands, policemen kill rather than arrest suspects and assassins, functioning as death squads.

Terrorism involves violence but is it an act of war? Once again we are confronted by a marked absence of consensus from the experts. The terrorist, however, is in no doubt. Obsessed by the need to establish his credentials through the recognition of his motives, the terrorist remains convinced that he is fighting a war. He sees himself as a soldier, even though he may wear no uniform, nor receive any formal training. The terrorist organisation may be ephemeral, and its members may accept minimum discipline, but they still see themselves as soldiers. Their weapons are the gun and the bomb, the battleground the city street and the objectives the vulnerable points of modern society.

Terrorism can indeed assume many of the characteristics we would more normally associate with conventional conflicts. Psychological warfare plays an important role where the aim is to demoralise the opposing forces, their government and the people on whom they count for support. Material destruction is high on the terrorist list of objectives. The destruction of resources communications and industry can paralyse the government. Such destruction can generate a sense of unease and uncertainty so that friends and others will withdraw their support, their capital and investments, and trade which may be the life blood of the nation's economic health will wither.

Military establishments worthy of the name have always found it difficult to look upon terrorism as a form of warfare. General Robert E. Lee said of the Confederacies' own guerrillas: 'I regard the whole system as an unmixed evil.' Evil or not, this form of conflict has been employed by many combatants through the ages, and disdaining terrorism will not make it go away. In some instances the professional soldier is the source of his own confusions. It is the authors' experience on more than one occasion when in the company of senior officers to have been told that the men under the officers' command were in a 'state of war' with the terrorists in Northern Ireland. Though doubtless still looking askance at unconventional warfare and its response, the military establishments have been forced, by circumstance, to accept the responsibility of their profession of arms in dealing with terrorism. The British, Americans, Israelis, French, South Africans and the Russians in both Eastern Europe and Afghanistan have been so engaged. Reality has legitimised the bastard.

There are others who would find great offence with this argument. They would maintain that the terrorists are not guerrillas because they are irregular soldiers who wage war on conventional military forces. Terrorism instead blurs the distinction between combatants and civilians, the separation of which is the central tenet of the laws of war. The latter sets out to identify and to define what is a crime, so that even in the confusions of combat, belligerents know what is lawful and what is unlawful in war.

Terrorists want both to have their cake and to eat it. They will not make distinctions or choices in targets and fail to discriminate between 'legitimate military targets' and civilians. Nevertheless they demand that their victims discriminate and accord them a status which separates them from the common criminal when captured. The British government's vacillations over this issue in Northern Ireland have not made the job of the Security Forces any easier, nor have they contributed to a settlement of the crisis.

'One man's floor is another man's ceiling, one man's terrorist is another man's freedom fighter' was an expression which had some validity in the years following the Second World War. It was a time when leaders of terrorist organisations, upon the defeat of their colonial masters, assumed the dignity of heads of state. Given that the Israeli leadership can trace its past to a time when it fought against the British, it is understandable why it in turn reacts so violently to the Palestinian threat.

There are still parts of the world where subject peoples suffer a high degree of alienation and repression from government, where inequalities and discrimination reside, and where the individual feels impotent against government and big business. In some instances political offence symbolises the little person's last remaining power to be noticed. The terrorist can carry the message of many others who feel aggrieved and who lack the opportunity to be heard. Frustrated without the means to act on events, the revolutionary will choose terror. These considerations have to be recognised, not as a justification for terrorism, but rather a means of explanation.

The fact that racial, linguistic, ethnic and religious antagonisms also promote violence is not going to help us to cope with terrorism. All that it does is to present us with a stark reality: until we root out the fundamental causes, terrorism can never be eradicated. In the meanwhile one answer is to avoid the trouble spots, but they are widespread, and as in the case of the TWA incident, the terrorists hijacked the flight in Europe to the Middle East.

It is reasonable to assume that when the Islamic Fundamentalists and Militias chased the United States out of the Lebanon, they did not stop at the shore of the Mediterranean, but followed the task force all the way home. There are probably Islamic extremists, 'sleepers', in the United States, awaiting the clarion call to take their holy war, through acts of terrorism, onto the front porches of Middle America. The United States, in seeking to take the war to the terrorists, has made too many enemies for it to be otherwise.

In a sense, the threat from the terrorist is now probably greater than ever, whether at home or abroad. Hijacks are back in vogue because the terrorist is better at getting weapons onto planes than we are at detecting him. Terrorism now includes a breed of men and women who do not care whether they live or die, so they will commit audacious acts against intolerable odds. Yet there is no real consensus and little by way of common language on terrorism, and we are invariably left with more questions than answers.

One sign of the concern expressed by both the public and the commercial sectors are the lavishly funded institutions and think tanks which have emerged on both sides of the Atlantic to study terrorism. Yet we are still hampered by the emotive quality of terrorist violence, and with every justification when such an act is perpetrated in a free and democratic society. Some of the new institutions amass, analyse and publish volumes of statistics, which seem to be of little general utility beyond the closeted discipline of research. There are statistics freely available which will reveal that out of the last 45 kidnappings, 18 ended in the death of the hostages. This does not tell us very much about the 46th kidnapping. However, a statistic which shows that the terrorist has a close on 90 per cent chance of escaping with his life in the event of a kidnap does clearly show that the next incident is never far away.

NOTE

1. Raymond Aron, *Century of Total War* (London: Derek Verschoyle, 1984).

3 The Terrorist Battleground

Terrorism is employed by small bands, rather than large organisations with extensive popular support. It is, so we are led to believe, the weapon of the weak, which is of little comfort to the victims of such an attack. Terrorism is the deliberate and systematic murder, maiming and menacing of the innocent to inspire fear for political ends. These days it has become less of an isolated threat or phenomenon of local fanatics, and increasingly part of a new international strategy resorted to by the enemies of freedom and the Western world. There are indeed very few places where one can travel which are completely free of a terrorist threat, and those that are present the visitor with another range of problems, namely those associated with a terrorist regime. In 1983 the United States lost more lives through international terrorism than in the previous 15 years put together. An analysis of the 1984 statistics show that 4000 people were killed and more than 4000 injured by 125 terrorist groups known to be operating worldwide, but principally in 50 countries.

Bombs are responsible for most terrorist incidents. The reason why this weapon is so popular is not difficult to discern. Bombs are easy to construct and easy to conceal. With one or two notable exceptions terrorists have no desire to die, and the bomb has the distinct advantage of not requiring their presence when it is detonated. Even so, the bomb has a couple of disadvantages. Homemade bombs are unstable and unpredictable, even when constructed by experts, and many terrorists are not. The second highest group of bomb victims are terrorists themselves – what the security forces gleefully describe as 'own goals'.

Telephone callers usually claim credit for bombings; invariably more than one for each incident. This means that hard evidence implicating individuals or groups is elusive, which can work in the terrorist's favour; but more often than not the instigators want the credit. In cases where a terrorist campaign is prolonged, such as in Northern Ireland, an elaborate series of codes are arranged between the terrorists and the Security Forces. Communication between the opposing forces is essential, particularly in the case of a telephoned warning, where the terrorist and the security forces have a vested interest in the preservation of life. It will do the former's cause no good if he kills too many of his own nationals too often. The bomb threat is intended to disrupt and inconvenience, not necessarily to kill and to maim.

With so many terrorist groups in existence, carrying their war to almost a third of the states that comprise our world, security forces are hard put at times to identify those who are responsible for an incident. The solution to the terrorist war lies in part in sound and effective intelligence, for it is only by such means that the menace can be countered. The more that is known about terrorism and terrorist organisations the easier it becomes to place the threat into its context, and to cope with the problem.

There are some of course who prefer not to know, but would rather place their safety in the hands of blind providence, but most businessmen and people whose work requires travel are better prepared if they understand something of the nature of the threat. We are up against 125 groups which operate in 50 countries and more. But is there some way in which we can distinguish between the terrorists and their battlegrounds? An obvious distinction is to separate the terrorists into Right and Left of the political spectrum. The Left of course have a long tradition in the history of terrorism, and 'big business' in terms both of property and of personnel is a favourite target for their bombs, extortion threats and assassinations. But any close study will reveal that terrorism of the Right has a long history, especially when labelled with the tag of nationalism. The Right are more likely to target people and organisations who are in sympathy with the Left, but this does not mean that big business is immune. Rabid nationalists frequently take exception to the presence of large foreign enterprises which they target as 'exploiters', or because such enterprises support, albeit tacitly, the government in power, to which they are probably ideologically opposed in the first instance.

The application of such labels may have some meaning in Europe, but further afield, and certainly beyond the Middle East, they have little relevance. Terrorist groups amongst the Palestinians or from Southern Africa may embrace the language of socialism in their message, but this is largely rhetorical; their prime objective is nationalism. Thus the groups will accept support from Moscow and from the West, as both have found to their cost.

There is a clear distinction which can be made if we apply

ideology in a different fashion. Organisations like the Red Army Faction (RAF), the Baader-Meinhof Group in West Germany, the Italian Red Brigades and the Weathermen in the United States, are very much isolated elitist conspiracies who emerged out of a strongly biased left-wing ideological and intellectual opposition to the State. All such groups in true Left tradition target big business and the visible symbols of western capitalism. In contrast the Basque ETA, FLQ in Quebec, the IRA and its derivatives, together with the multifarious Palestinian organisations, are often referred to as 'Terrorists of the Blood'. They are primarily nationalist, and cannot survive without the support of the population. This support is given because a set of political circumstances prevail where ordinary people, who are by no means violent normally, now believe that only a violent opposition to the state will achieve their interests. The people are deeply imbued with a sense of the history of their grievance, and probably with a powerful religious influence too, and they will continue to support the men of violence. No matter what security measures are adopted, and in the case of Northern Ireland there is very little left to try, none will succeed until the problem is tackled at its roots.

The Palestinian terrorists, ETA and the IRA are a reflection of a set of political circumstances rather than an independent manifestation of irrational violence such as the Red Brigades. Their targets are those who seem to support what they regard as the 'occupying powers'; and since this is never defined precisely almost everybody is at risk. Such indiscriminate and random action has come increasingly to be associated with the activities of 'Islamic Jihad'. This is the name used by those responsible for the horrific attacks on American and French peacekeeping forces in the Lebanon, the piracy of the Italian cruise liner *Achille Lauro*, and a spate of recent hijackings. Experts have still to agree on the precise identity of this shadowy organisation. 'Islamic Jihad' means 'Holy War for Islam' and some would maintain that it comprises a number of semi autonomous groups all dedicated to furthering the cause of militant Shi-ite fundamentalism.

International Terrorism of the Palestinian and Islamic varieties captures the headlines, and it is all too easy to ignore the local or indigenous terrorist threat, especially in Western Europe and Latin America. The record over recent years stands in stark testimony to the efficacy of these movements. Armenians brought down one government in Turkey, while Basque ETA has shaken another in

Spain. In Italy and in Northern Ireland, particularly throughout the 1970s, the terrorist threats challenged the very fibre of government.

Since 1977 indigenous terrorist organisations have been responsible for over 5000 deaths in Western Europe, and have soured and strained relations between states which are otherwise close friends and allies. The Northern Ireland question is a source of mutual irritability between London and Washington, and undermines relations with Eire. France and Spain quarrel over the Basques. In all these instances terrorism subverts and undermines the fabric of the Western Alliance which seeks to unite Western Europe and bind it to the United States in a common stance against the Soviet and Warsaw Pact threat.

Now in more recent years a new form of indigenous terrorism has emerged to plague the cities of the Western World. It is frequently referred to as 'soft terrorism', so named because in democratic societies the voices of protest have been directed towards the protection of animals, and particularly those used in experiments. Animal Rights Liberation movements have targeted pharmaceutical companies, medical laboratories, the cosmetics and confectionery industry. Installations have been bombed, animals released and in some instances eminent scientists attacked. The threat of product contamination has become an increasingly favourite weapon of extortion by criminals, and when direct action by animal rights movements is included, the problem for industry can only get worse.

In Western Europe local or indigenous terrorist activity is an actual or political threat for most countries. Spain, Italy, Turkey, France and Northern Ireland occupy the front line because terrorists have caused considerable casualties and damage, and provoked governments to deploy their armed forces in support of the local means of law and order which can no longer cope with the scale of the programme. In West Germany, Belgium, Portugal and Greece the terrorist threat is on a more limited though still a dangerous scale. Other countries, such as the Netherlands, experience terrorist 'flare ups' on a spasmodic scale with, for example, the South Moluccan extremists grabbing the headlines in 1975–8. The spate of terrorism which hit Italy and West Germany with Baader-Meinhof and the Red Brigades in the forefront was largely reduced to manageable proportions in the later 1970s after strenuous efforts on the part of Government and the Security Forces. For a while at least Europe was quiet and the intelligence and security forces were rightly proud of their success until a new wave of terrorism swept across the region taking everyone by surprise.

A European 'brotherhood of terrorism' seems to have replaced the divided threat formerly posed by separate groups, which had largely confined their activity to targets within their own borders. This form of international terrorism is 'violence for effect'. The movement seeks to create the impression that the terrorist groups are able to strike with impunity. Small, usually numerically weak bands attempt to become a credible threat by demonstrating that the authorities are impotent when it comes to protecting their citizens from such outrages. Such terrorist incidents involve the target assassination or hostage-taking of notable figures such as government ministers, senior representatives of the establishment, and prominent industrialists. This campaign is accomplished by bombing operations, with government ministries, military installations, and commercial and industrial sites as their main targets.

There is a dearth of hard evidence, but such information as is available indicates that this new breed of terrorism, which the West German Security Agencies have labelled 'the Third Generation', has learned from the mistakes made by those groups which first bombed and assassinated their way to notoriety in Europe. For one thing, they are better organised, operating in small secure cells that are by all accounts exceedingly difficult to penetrate.

The amorphous relationship among the criminal core of an underground organisation and others who may be associated with the subversives across a wide spectrum of seemingly innocent occupations presents the intelligence agencies with a major problem. Simply to trace the connecting links which might explain and help unravel the functions and machinations of terror organisation can take months if not years to collate.

The 'third generation' have adopted a cellular organisation which is designed to thwart the most sophisticated intelligence techniques. They are able to exercise command control and co-ordination in a rigid, tight-knit, self-contained structure. This allows them to operate with considerable impunity in democracies where individual freedoms are preserved and codified. The ability of the intelligence and security agencies to penetrate clandestine and subversive organisations, are circumscribed by law. This can explain in part why the recent record of the agencies, especially in West Germany, has been so dismal. In January 1985 Dr Herbert Hillenbroick, Head of the Federal Republic's counterterrorist unit, admitted publicly: 'I will be quite honest: neither the police nor the state attorney's office, nor we ourselves are in a position to get the RAF under control.'

It is the very nature of the terrorist brotherhood which lies at the root of the problem. It appears that at least five groups have formed an alliance. In January 1985 the Red Army Faction (RAF) and Action Directe (AD) formally announced they were 'teaming up' to strike against NATO targets, and against France's military ties with the North Atlantic Alliance. At the same time Forças Populares 25 de Abril (FP25) made a mortar attack on a NATO naval squadron anchored in Lisbon harbour.

Within the month police chiefs and counterterrorist experts met at the Council of Ministers building of the European Community in Brussels. Their task was to devise a common approach to this new plague of 'Euro-terrorism'. The candidly honest West Germans were no longer alone, for their European partners came to the unanimous conclusion that they too were ill-equipped to deal with the problem.

The police chiefs and security agencies have not always been helped by their political masters. Jean-Marc Rouillan and Nathalie Menignon were among the founder members of Action Directe. Both had been arrested by the French police in September 1980, but were released a year later under an amnesty proclaimed by President Mitterrand following his election success. The pardon infuriated the French police at the time, and it is one which the President and the Administration have already come to regret. As soon as Menignon and Rouillan were released, they embarked upon a series of bank robberies across France, presumably to refinance AD before fleeing across the border to the relative sanctuary of Brussels. They chose Belgium because at the time it was a safe haven for terrorists. The Belgian government had the quaint notion that a terrorist was somebody who attacked targets of the country in which he was domiciled; whereas if he attacked targets in other countries then he was a freedom fighter. So while other European governments tried to tackle the problem, Brussels refused to be involved, granting immunity to anyone provided that they did not misbehave. Thus Menignon and Rouillon had plenty of opportunity to meet in Brussels with the terrorist community, and it was there that the new alliance was born.

In June 1984, 800 kilos of plastic explosive were stolen from a site in Brussels. These were used to bomb targets in Germany, France and Belgium. There was also an agreement, amounting to a joint strategy over targets, with European subsidiaries of American conglomerates involved in the defence field appearing high on the hit list. Litton, Man and Honeywell were three high-tech companies singled out for attention early in the new bombing campaign.

Belgium too reaped the reward of its Government's naivety; for one of the most startling developments has been the emergence of Communist Combatant Cells (CCC), the country's own terrorist group. It struck first at NATO targets such as pipelines and supply bases. More recently CCC has attacked Litton, Man and Honeywell's premises in Belgium. Despite the plethora of attractive targets in Belgium, with the Headquarters of NATO, SHAPE (its military arm) and the European Community's Commission offices all located in and around the capital, the police had neither the facilities nor the expertise to deal with the rash of incidents.

Neither were the Italians immune. Their security agencies had known as early as 1981 of ties between the surviving remnants of the Red Brigade, France's Action Directe and the Red Army Faction. Rome shared their intelligence with the authorities in Paris and Bonn, both of whom dismissed the reports as 'alarmist'. As late as February 1985 the Italians were publicly highly critical of the French. The Defence Minister Giovanni Spadolini vigorously upbraided France for 'sheltering a terrorist multinational' capable of striking throughout Europe. Such indignation did conceal cant and hypocrisy. Earlier in the 1970s the Italian government of the day concluded a sensitive, highly secret deal with Palestinian terrorists. In return for financial assistance and sanctuary in Italy, the Palestinians agreed not to attack targets in Italy, or Alitalia's (the state's airline) planes or flights. The Italians kept their end of the bargain, the Palestinians did not. It then all leaked out, much to the embarrassment of the administration.

The Euro-terrorists are anxious to prove that their movements have not been defeated, and this may be the main reason behind the spate of bombings. The fact, too, that so many of the attacks are aimed at military and defence-related targets suggests a second objective. There is no evidence to suggest that their campaign is directed by Moscow, but it cannot be denied that the terrorist operations rather neatly serve the Soviet's current anti-NATO, anti-Cruise campaign.

The Euro-terrorists have turned Europe into a battleground which has further been ravaged by the numerous international groups and factions which have chosen to operate there. International terrorism is distinguished by three characteristics. As with other forms of terrorism it embodies an act, whether it be assassination or kidnapping, extortion or arson, which is essentially criminal in nature. Secondly, international terrorism is politically motivated. An extremist political group, convinced of the rightness of its cause, will resort to violence and thereby unleash attacks in which innocent deaths become a calculated pressure-shock objective. Finally the terrorist will operate over national frontiers and even across continents to draw attention to the cause.

The Palestinians spring immediately to mind in any discussion of international terrorism; but why do they chose Europe? Logistically Western Europe is an ideal region for such terrorist campaigns. Unable to penetrate into Israel, which is the Palestinians' primary target, because of the quality and efficiency of the counterterrorist forces, Europe at least in geographical terms seems to be the next best thing. There are large ethnic communities of Palestinians living there who can provide cover and support for operations. Europe is geographically compact. It has excellent transport and communication facilities, and movement across frontiers especially by land is relatively uncomplicated. There is a preponderance of attractive, symbolically important targets: Jewish and American establishments and prominent personalities. Commercial enterprises and embassies proliferate, which allows much wider choice for target selection and overstretches the resources of the security forces, who simply cannot begin to provide effective cover and protection. Finally, and most important of all, the publicity spotlight is brighter and more intense in Western Europe than anywhere else in the world with the possible exception of certain parts of the United States. Europe offers instant media exposure: newspapers, journals, radio and television saturate the region.

For the international terrorist, publicity above all else is their primary tactical consideration. Other parts of the world can offer some of these advantages, but only Western Europe can offer the lot, and it is for this reason that it has become such a magnet for international terrorism. With the possible exception of the Lebanon, the Western business executive is more at risk in Europe than anywhere else. The international terrorist can also count on the support of those regimes which are prepared to abuse their diplomatic privileges by providing logistical back-up and support. The European embassies of such renegade regimes as Libya, South

Yemen, Syria, Iran and Cuba act as the paymasters for such terrorist groups. Europe, too, has witnessed more than its fair share of state-directed terrorist activities. There was the much publicised assassination attempt on His Holiness the Pope in which, despite all the confusions, actions by Bulgaria and the Soviet Union have still to be explained.

Iran, Syria and Libya in particular have used this variant of international terrorism to silence and intimidate exiled political dissidents, and serve their own foreign policy needs. The Syrians have little desire or use for a Palestinian state, despite its support for Palestinian liberation. Damascus has ambitions to see a Greater Syria established in the Middle East, which would involve the integration of present-day Lebanon, Syria, Jordan, pre-Israel Palestine, Iraq, Kuwait and some observers would include Cyprus too. The Syrians use their favourite terrorist group, the Syrian Socialist Nationalist Party, to further their aims. Abu Nidal, the notorious Palestinian terrorist leader who masterminded the massacres at Rome and Vienna airports in December 1981, the 'Achille Lauro' and many other incidents espouses the Syrian cause. Thus the presence in Europe of terrorists and sympathetic embassies attracts intelligence agencies and provokes antiterrorist measures. The Israelis have been specially active in taking the war of revenge to the Palestinians; but in the crowded streets and thoroughfares of Europe's capitals.

Some states use terrorism as an instrument of foreign policy when it is directed at a hostile power. The Gulf War has spawned a terrorist mini war between Iran and Iraq. European companies importing arms to Iraq have been the target of Iranian terrorist attacks. Libya has pursued its quarrels with the United States by bombing American property and installations in Europe. Terrorism thus becomes an appropriate technology for the warfare of the weak; for Libya is in no position to challenge the vastly superior power of the United States in any conventional military fashion.

Terrorism comes in many shapes and sizes, and it can be found almost anywhere in the world. Revolutionary violence in the Middle East, whether Palestinian, Islamic or pan-Arab in its objectives, routinely turns to terror as an extension of war by other means. The resort to terror is ubiquitous, witnessed for example by the horrors of the Lebanese conflict, now twelve years old. Terrorism is particularly prevalent in liberal democracies where the terrorist in the most cynical of fashions makes use of the very virtues of the state he is seeking to subvert. Terrorism thrives in weak dictatorships or inefficient totalitarian regimes. At the time of writing, President Pinochet in Chile appears to be under siege from indigenous terrorist opposition to his harsh but ineffectual regime. Terrorism does not 'occur' in efficient totalitarian regimes such as the Soviet Union and throughout much of the Eastern Bloc. This does not mean that the Russians never experience terrorist attacks; given their unhappy mix of nationalities and ethnic groups there is bound to be unrest which provokes political violence. However, Moscow controls the media, and distills information and news both internally and for foreign consumption, so it is as if such incidents never occurred.

Indigenous, transnational and international groups operate within a network of interlocking agreements and understandings, offering mutual support on operations. Even more sinister is evidence which shows terrorist groups combining with organised crime to mount operations. Such joint enterprises occur especially in extortions and bank raids. In recent years Western Europe, the Middle East and Latin America have accounted for close to three-quarters of all terrorist activity. Of these Western Europe is the most active environment simply because of its geography and its unique confrontation with multilayered terrorist activity.

Part II

The Threat

4 The Psychology of Terrorism

Terrorism is not rampant, but it is more prevalent than one imagines. Terrorists kill, maim and torture. Their victims may be children in a school, travellers like those at Rome, Vienna or Karachi, holiday-makers on the *Achille Lauro* or high-profile industrialists en route from home to the office. A terrorist's victim can be anyone; a businessman abroad has no particular political identity, but he can be kidnapped, maimed or simply blown to bits.

Where it does occur, terrorism attacks the very basic safety and security needs of a country. Unless these needs are satisfied, the people will find themselves living in a state of constant fear from the terrorist, and disaffection with the authorities who are powerless to protect them. If people do not feel safe, they cannot grow individually or achieve their true potential. A classic example occurred in the aftermath of the American air raids on Libya. Many Americans feared reprisals if they came to Europe, and so cancelled their vacations. This was a completely irrational action since their chances of becoming involved in a terrorist incident were sufficiently remote, and all sorts of bizarre statistics were quoted by interested parties. But stay away they did and this in turn hit the European tourist industry and placed many people's livelihood at risk. Though Colonel Qaddafi could not have foreseen the effects his threats would produce, it is nevertheless a salutary lesson in psychological warfare at work.

Elite movements aside, terrorists cannot survive without the support of the population and that support is given for many reasons, but at least in part it is a response to a set of political and social circumstances. Ordinary people who are by no means bloodthirsty come to believe the terrorist message that only through some form of violent opposition can their interests be protected. The polarisation of attitudes in Southern Lebanon and the subsequent emergence of Islamic Jihad onto the international scene is a case in point.

Psychological warfare is basically about influencing the 'hearts and minds' of a population. In the psychologist's jargon it relates to *cognition* (what people think) and *affect* (what people feel). This in

43

turn influences their behaviour and subsequently that of a whole segment of society. Let us examine this in a little more detail. Terrorism is about undermining the confidence a population has in the ability of the government of the day to provide a safe environment in which people can live a comfortable existence without fearing for their lives or livelihood. Thus terrorism is about confidence, it is an attack on the morale of a population and operates at a very basic human level. The psychologist Abraham Maslow put forward the idea of the hierarchy of needs as illustrated in Figure 4.1.

1   Knowledge
2   Self-actualisation
3   Love
4   Safety
5   Basic physical needs

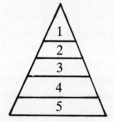

Figure 4.1   Maslow's hierarchy of needs

Unless the basic needs at the bottom of the hierarchy are satisfied, notably those of safety and security; it is impossible for the human being to aspire to higher activity such as gaining knowledge; and that all-important state of 'self actualisation' where the individual becomes totally in tune with his environment and achieves his full potential.

Psychologists traditionally tend to consider human functioning in terms of the individual's thinking, feeling and doing. Terrorism is particularly sinister in that it affects the 'feeling' area of an individual. Indeed it is based on the very concept of producing maximum emotional impact, sorrow and pity for the victims and anger against the authorities for allowing the terrorists to operate. The key to producing this emotional effect is, of course, the media impact value of the terrorist act.

In psychological warfare it is important to identify the target population. This not only means understanding their nature, beliefs, values and so on, but more particularly their fears and anxieties, their weaknesses and vulnerabilities. What the authorities have failed to appreciate, for example in the case of Islamic Jihad, is that radical fundamentalists constitute a small minority in most Muslim societies (Iran is the exception) and they are embattled. Fear is also the key to the fundamentalists' attitudes towards non-Muslims; the greater they perceive a threat to be the more intense their hostility.

Whatever their motivation, terrorists will choose as the target one specific group for the threat of violence, usually on geographical grounds, such as individuals in an enclosed space – a theatre, shopping precinct or aircraft. These are the secondary victims. The primary victims, namely the entire population, are targeted via the media for effect. The essence of the terrorist's penumbra of fear is that no one can be safe from his danse macabre. In the summer of 1985 TWA Flight 874 helplessly ferried its 158 captives around the Mediterranean after being hijacked by two Shia extremists. The United States then endured seventeen days of prime-time humiliation before the last of the hostages were released.

One of the most significant features about the growth of terrorist activity in recent years has been the sharp increase in the incidence of hostage taking. Most often victimised are, in descending order, citizens of the United States, France, the United Kingdom, West Germany and Italy, which together account for just over half the incidents. Now hostages can be taken in a variety of ways: solo, as in a targeted kidnap; or in groups, as in a hijacked airliner; but all can experience a variety of psychological problems which range from stress-related heart attacks to long-term identification with their captors.

Hostages primarily fall into three categories. Firstly there is the person of special value who becomes the target of a particular terrorist group and is abducted either for the political publicity to the cause, or to demand a large ransom (and perhaps both). In some cases, such victims have been murdered in the very early stages, perhaps as a revenge killing, or to make a political point. More usually the victim is worth very much more to the terrorist group alive, though death can still be the end result if, as in the case of Aldo Moro, they have served their purpose.

The second type of victim is the one who is caught up in a planned situation, and is taken as an expedient hostage. The classic example is the passenger of an aircraft which is hijacked, unlucky enough to be at the wrong place at the wrong time. The victim has little value other than simply being a human asset; his identity is not important. Even so the expedient hostage is at risk and it can have tragic consequences. An American Serviceman was killed, and in a most brutal fashion, on the TWA flight hijacked to Beirut; but perhaps it could be argued that this man, a member of a Special Forces Unit, had a special value. Mr Leo Klinghoffer had no 'special value'. He was a passenger on the *Achille Lauro* murdered by the terrorists presumably as they sought to assert their authority. In a most brutal fashion this incident pinpointed just how different cultures often fail to appreciate how others will perceive their behaviour. It is quite clear in many people's minds that Leo Klinghoffer was chosen to be killed because he was disabled, not because he was Jewish. To the terrorist he was a man in a wheelchair, an elderly person of little value. Yet it was the fact that he was disabled that so outraged Western societies, that gave the act of murder an added dimension of callous brutality.

The third type of incident is when the victim is taken as an expedient in an unplanned situation. This tends to be associated more with criminal than with terrorist activities, where a robbery has been discovered. It is really outside the scope of this book but it is worth pointing out that as technology speeds up the response time of police forces, we are likely to experience an increase in the 'crime in progress' hostage incident.

Whenever hostages are involved, the victims are placed in a highly stressful, traumatic and most hazardous situation. At the same time hostage seizures are extremely tense situations that tax the abilities and resources of even the most sophisticated and skilled governments. Human beings respond to such traumatic experiences in a fairly well defined sequence of phases. The manner of victim response to a terrorist attack depends upon the nature of the incident, whether it be a bombing, aircraft hijack, kidnap attempt, or whatever. However, those individuals who are aware of the response phases are undoubtedly better able to cope with the situation, because they can *intellectualise* the experience and retain a measure of control rather than become swamped by the experience.

Many of the studies of the victims' experience are modelled on the theory of rape trauma. The bomb incident is in many respects similar to rape. The victim is suddenly subjected to violence, but the event is usually shortlived, and most of the victim's reactions relate to coping with the aftermath. The hijack, siege or kidnap, in contrast, is a protracted situation which may last weeks, months or even years. In this context hostages have much in common with prisoners, both criminal and wartime; except that for the hostage captivity is usually totally unexpected.

Let us consider a generalised model of a victim of a protracted terrorist incident and we will use as our example a terrorist siege in an embassy. The event begins when the terrorists declare themselves and establish that normal activity is disrupted. The normal reaction of those hapless individuals caught inside the building – whether staff or visitors, they are all now hostages – is that of utter disbelief. This is a most dangerous time. In psychological terms, the hostage takers could be said to be in a state of emotional erection. They are frightened; though the adrenalin is pumping and excitement is high, they are akin to cornered animals, ready to fight to the death, and to kill anyone who challenges their authority or their purpose.

The hostages survive by keeping calm, even though some will suffer injuries which will all add to the effects of the shock. Escape is usually impossible if the terrorists have any degree of competence. Other influences come into play. Time distortions often occur and the victims feel numb for they are quite suddenly no longer in control of their own situations. Someone else has invaded their lives and controls their destinies. The term 'idiocide' has often been used to describe this condition of relating to the 'death of the self'. In simple terms, the victim has encountered someone who is bigger, stronger and better armed, who damages and assaults him. As a result of such aggression the hostage feels less powerful than normal, more fearful and is pushed down a couple of rungs on what the sociologists might describe as the 'dominance hierarchy'. Much of this initial stage of denial or disbelief is due to a natural suppression by the brain of environmental stimuli which, unless subdued, would cause the individual to experience an excessive stress reaction. It is a sort of natural anaesthetic, similar in many ways to the feelings experienced by someone who has just learned of the death of a loved one; without the numbness of the denial state, the situation would become unbearable.

After a while, things settle down somewhat, at least as much as they ever will in such a situation. The terrorists are in control and in contact with the authorities outside. The hostages come to realise that they are not to be executed as long as they obey their captors. This phase is called by some experts the disengagement of reality phase. The individual will try to disengage himself from his perception of reality by occupying his mind; counting the patterns on the wallpaper, for example. This is short-lived, for reality catches up and he is forced to adapt realistically to the predicament.

This is invariably accompanied by feelings of depression as he confronts the utter hopelessness of the situation.

Much thereafter will depend on whether the hostage begins to identify with, and form a sympathetic relationship with, the captors, or whether he rejects them out of hand, thereby reinforcing his own identity as the injured party. In the first instance the hostage is moving into the Stockholm Syndrome. Much as been written about this predicament, named after a bank raid which occurred in 1973 in Sweden. The bank raid was discovered in progress and a siege ensued. The hostages began to develop positive feelings towards their captors, generous men who allowed them to live. It was the police who were the enemy.

Like all generalised and psychological syndromes which catch the public imagination, Stockholm does need to be considered with care. Psychologists refer to it as the "Survival Identification Syndrome", and it does not occur on every occasion. It seems that the degree of isolation, the period of confinement and the interaction between the hostages and captors determine the degree to which the syndrome will develop. Frequently hostages do develop positive feelings towards their captors. At the same time, the captives often become disaffected with the authorities as they feel increasingly they have been abandoned. Part of the problem in assessing the validity of the Stockholm Syndrome is that hostages upon release invariably deny having suffered from the effect, despite the fact that they display all the symptoms.

In yet another version of the Stockholm Syndrome some of the hostages involved in the hijacking of TWA Flight 874 afterwards publicly attributed the cause of Lebanon's unending trauma more to the United States and Israel than to terrorism in its most unadorned form. So long as terrorist acts are given the illusion of reasoned discussion, terrorism will continue to exploit public sympathy. Terrorism breeds on success and therefore, sincere as the hostages may have been in their personal views, the best anti-terrorism response would have been silence.

Just as the hostages develop feelings towards their captors, the latter begin to appreciate that they are becoming increasingly dependent on their prisoners as assets with which to bargain. As captivity progresses, the hostages in effect regress to an almost childlike state, referred to as 'traumatic psychological infantilism'. They are dependent upon another human being, like a child to its mother. Some begin to model childlike behaviour, becoming compliant, submissive and attempting to ingratiate themselves with their captors. Such regression can cause all sorts of problems. Sexual attractions are aroused and stimulated; this occurred in the original Stockholm incident. Hostages have been known to impede rescue attempts and to hide their captors from the intervention troops, and others have refused to testify in subsequent trials, such is the force of this stress bonding effect. In extreme cases captives can experience severe attitudinal changes, where they can be 'brainwashed' into accepting totally new ideas and sets of values. Patty Hearst was a classic example: she eventually joined the terrorist group which had kidnapped her and participated in subsequent operations.

Of course this process of hostages forming bonds with their captors is very dependent on what actually takes place during the hostage incident, and particularly the release or escape phase. Hostages who have been subjected to maltreatment do not develop the Stockholm Syndrome as obviously as those who have been well treated by their captors. Likewise those hostages who escape as a result of a violent incident where subconsciously they realise that the terrorists would have killed them are less likely to experience positive feelings.

In the aftermath of a terrorist hijack or kidnap, there is considerable evidence to show that hostages will experience psychological problems in adjusting to normality. In particular they may experience sleep problems, flashbacks, feelings that they are being followed and general insecurity which can in some cases border on paranoia. There are several psychotherapeutic treatment programmes in existence to combat 'hostage after-effects', and this is a theme to which we will return later in the book. One of the most significant aspects of terrorist behaviour is that it places people under conditions which are inherently stressful. The hostage and kidnap incident is a traumatic experience because the victim is held captive and under the threat of injury or death. For many people in many places in the world there is the gnawing threat of living with danger on a daily basis. The threat of terrorist bomb or ambush and the fear generated by indiscriminate and brutalised soldiery is something which has to be faced on a day by day basis. It is the production of the stress reaction which is a particularly significant aspect of the terrorist's tactics and something in which he has become increasingly skilled and adept at exploiting in recent years.

What are the chances of surviving a hostage incident? In a recent analysis of forty-two kidnaps where all hostages were released, four elements were considered crucial:

The terrorists allowed outsiders to substitute for hostages.
The terrotists negotiated and set fewer deadlines.
Few of the events were barricade situations.
The terrorists did not demand the release of prisoners.

5 The Mind of the Terrorist

Since 1984, when they declared open season on Americans in Lebanon, Islamic Jihad have taken eleven as hostage. Terry Anderson, a 38-year-old Middle East Correspondent for Associated Press was kidnapped on 16 March 1985 in Beirut. He spent the first three weeks of his captivity lying chained to a bed, threatened with death if he uttered a single word. For six months this tough ex-Marine and Vietnam veteran withstood the onslaught of his captors during which time he was beaten, kicked and tormented.

Frank Reyer is an Engineering Professor at the American University in Beirut. When he was kidnapped he was blindfolded, tied and chained to a wall. He was told that if he moved he would be beaten, and hour after hour his tormenters would wait for the slightest twitch, when he was beaten without mercy. (At the time of writing both men, along with eight others and three Frenchmen, are still enduring the hell of their confinement.)

The terrorist sees himself as an individual who is seeking to redress for real or imagined grievances and can presumably justify or rationalise his behaviour as working towards a worthwhile end. He is not the first to live by the diktat that the end justifies the means, but what mental processes exist in the so-called mind of the terrorist, and how is it that people who appear outwardly normal can commit such dreadful acts of sadism? In order to understand this question we need to begin by looking at how normal judgements develop in the individual.

The psychologist maintains that our moral sense or code of values is developed through a three-part process. Firstly an individual does things on the basis of whether or not he/she will be rewarded for such behaviour. Thus a child will repeat behaviour for which he is praised and tend to discontinue those actions which lead to punishment, particularly if the latter fits the crime and is painful. At the second level of moral development the individual assesses the acceptability of a particular course of action according to a frame or reference; usually it is the law. Thus the 'normal' person does not immediately give way to animal urges, but will consider whether it is acceptable in terms of the law or other norms of behaviour. This obviously implies a tacit acceptance of or at least compliance with the rules and regulations of the social system in which he lives, even though the requirements of societies can differ considerably.

The third and final stage of moral development is the situation where a person will judge the acceptability of a particular course of action, not with regard to an external framework such as the law, but in relation to their own individual sense of what is right and wrong. The subject is exercising free choice, and in so doing may well indeed break the law. It is something we all do from time to time, by driving above the speed limit, failing to return a borrowed book or taking paper clips and stationery from the office. When we do these things we assess the acceptability of that action in accordance to our definitional framework, and at the same time rationalise our behaviour by excusing it against an overriding judgement, 'it's an unnecessary speed limit', or 'what's a few paper clips?' Thus an individual's behaviour can be considered in terms of his or her own set of underlying values which in turn influences the style in which he/she solves problems and his or her approach to relations with other people.

Is the terrorist no different? Does he rationalise his actions, even the most brutal by saying 'it is for the sake of the cause which is above all other considerations'? Is it sufficient to explain away his behaviour because by hiding behind a political banner he is able to carry out his deeds of violence? There are no empirical answers to these questions but perhaps the key is in his motivation. Comparisons are often made between terrorists and criminals. Terrorists use criminal acts to work towards their declared objectives, and criminals often use terror tactics for personal gain. The gulf between the two is significant, for the terrorist the cause is everything but for the criminal wealth and profit is the motivation.

Terrorism, as we have already seen, involves two sets of victims so the violence occurs in a triangular relationship. In contrast, there is just the criminal and his victim in their bipolar world. Criminals frequently work alone, whereas the terrorist invariably is part of a group and its influence over the individual is very significant in shaping terrorist actions. The terrorist has been described as an actor, playing a part to an audience in a 'theatre of terror'. He or she is thus very concerned with image. Indeed for many it is the fact of being a terrorist, rather than the declared political objectives, which becomes the primary motivating factor. In circumstances such as these, terrorists degenerate into what the experts refer to as 'activity orientated' individuals rather than the more noble 'goal oriented'. For these people it is the 'doing' rather than the 'arriving' which becomes all-important, especially for those with psychopathic tendencies. In this context the role of the media assumes a new significance in the manner in which they report or portray a terrorist incident. It has an impact not just on the group who have perpetrated the act but can also influence others who may seek similar glory through emulation or role modelling.

Is there a difference in terrorist behaviour on the part of men and women? The male seeks violent behaviour as an extension of the aggressive pseudo-delinquent stage of his normal development. It is, so we are told, a natural extension under appropriate circumstances of environmental pressures for the male to extend his behaviour from minor violence into full scale killing. Military training systems have long recognised this fact and many states have survived largely as a result of their ability to turn citizens into an effective army when the need arises. It is different for a female. To become violent requires that she deviates more sharply from the norm than is the case of the male. Thus the woman who becomes a terrorist will be likely to have experienced a more traumatic mental adjustment than the male, whose approach to killing can be graduated or progressive.

Probably the most interesting approach to the human mind which is relevant to the terrorist situation is contained in basic Freudian psychology. Freud suggested that the mind operates at two levels, the conscious, of which the person is aware, and the subconscious. In practice our behaviour is determined by three interacting competent parts of the mind, all of which operate within the conscious–subconscious framework. Freud maintained that the most animal or basic part of the mind is the *id*, which consists of our drives for food, air, water, sexual satisfaction and other appetites. This is the beast within us, long recognised as such and used in many a successful defence in courts of law, of which the French *crime passionelle* is the most notorious.

At a higher plane exists the *ego* which seeks to satisfy these needs in a reasonably conformist fashion and formulates realistic plans for their accomplishment. This too can sometimes become distorted, or get out of phase and work in other directions as witnessed by the oft cited criminal mind and other forms of deviant behaviour. The third aspect of the mind is the *superego* which is a kind of conscience, keeping watch over the other two. Freud argued that these three components of the mind exist in conflict with each other, and that the mind is sufficiently resourceful to produce defence mechanisms which help to resolve such problems. These mechanisms include regression, repression and sublimation. Rationalisation might be used by a terrorist to justify a killing or bombing on the grounds that it is for the 'cause'. Would these considerations allow us to assume that terrorists are people who behave the way they do because their minds have gone wrong? The Freudian model indeed implies a malfunction, namely that the *superego's control over the id* has failed.

There is ample evidence, however, to suggest that the terrorist mind operates within the bounds of moral psychology rather than displaying signs of mental illness which can be diagnosed by orthodox psychiatric methods. Terrorists are intelligent, fit, usually well trained and highly motivated individuals when it comes to working for the 'cause'. What they are doing, at least in the early stages of terrorist association, is exposing dissidence according to a continuum, rather than indulging in any psychopathic behaviour. It is unusual for a terrorist to become a terrorist spontaneously. More often it is the case that an individual is drawn by stages into a terrorist group, perhaps beginning in a minor supporting role on the fringes such as distributing leaflets. Thereafter there is a gradual progression through such activities as acting as a courier into the centre of activity and escalating violence. In some terrorist groups, and especially the guerrilla, freedom-fighter movements, this could be a ritualistic affair with initiations based on tribal customs for new recruits. In others, initiation is through some test of initiative or loyalty which involves a criminal act and thereby exerts a blackmailing element from which there is no turning back.

As an individual, the would-be terrorist has often been rejected in some fashion by society and tends to be a loner. It is human nature to be part of the group, and so the alienated loner, who regards himself as a failure, is naturally drawn towards any group which will not only accept him, but also provide the ways and means to 'kick back' at the system which has rejected him. This is a well-known ploy and is used by the Soviet KGB to lure spinster secretaries in government ministries or military headquarters where they have access to secrets. It is used by terrorists who set up front organisations in universities to attract those whom their specially trained operatives recognise as the 'walking wounded' in the popularity stakes. What can the psychologist tell us about the personality traits or the 'mind set' of the terrorist? Is there a personality profile of the terrorist? What sort of personality is it who can commit outrageous acts of violence, face to face or anonymously and without any apparent sense of guilt?

There doesn't appear to be a standard personality trait in this instance, but certain types of personalities of the more extreme kind are drawn towards terrorist behaviour as with other forms of violence. These would include the angry paranoid, the stimulus seeking psychopath and the self absorbed individual who is self-centred, concerned only with himself and who cares nothing for the feelings of other people. If there is a generalisation to be made in view of the nature of terrorist violence it would appear that terrorists are primarily people with disorders of affect (feelings towards others in particular) and yet competent as regards cognition and behaviour. They often have a tendency to externalise problems, and project their own inadequacies onto others. The terrorist, for example, will blame the government for promoting violence through its countermeasures, whereas it is the terrorist violence which in the first instance prompted such a response. Part of his strategy is to provoke the authorities into over-reaction, thereby acting as a catalyst to gain further recruits for the cause.

There are no terrorist types. They are individuals alienated in some fashion and drawn to a group that accepts them and gives them an identity. So it is the group which exerts the influence over the behaviour of the individual, and particularly in the case of terrorists. The terrorist group is clandestine and covert, so cohesion figures more prominently than in other groups. It functions under highly stressful conditions and its thinking, both the individual's and the group's, can easily become warped or impaired.

Psychologists who have studied group behaviour believe that a terrorist group, because it is under such pressure, can feel vulnerable, and will indulge in excessive risk-taking to achieve its objectives. This is particularly true of those terrorists inspired by radical Shia fundamentalism. Fear is the key to fundamentalist attitudes towards non-Muslims from whom they are totally alienated. The greater they perceive the threat to be, the more intense their hostility and audacious their behaviour. They are not particularly sophisticated. Their tactics seem to be a reversion to an earlier style of terrorism witnessed twenty years ago where the aim was simply to inflict as many casualties as possible and draw maximum media attention; but a proven willingness to use violence and a determination to succeed frequently makes them proof against conventional security precautions. When this is allied to the suicidal commitment of the

Shia, whose religious traditions of martyrdom and protest are so much more amenable to terrorism, they present a formidable threat. They are children of Lebanon's civil war generation, recruited from the street gangs of Beirut, and they have little to lose. They are men and women with a readiness to die which is always the deadly strength of the fanatic. The world is against them and all they seek is release into paradise in bloody spectaculars.

In instances such as these, and even in more 'rational' terrorist behaviour where the members still aim to survive, the individual is totally immersed in the group, his ego becomes the group ego. The group will believe its own fantasy, the fantasy war it is fighting against 'the enemy'. If the authorities respond in a violent fashion, this simply reinforces the fantasy and the myth, and the group becomes even more cohesive.

Thus the psychologist advises counterterrorist strategies which do not stress violent responses and thereby reinforce the fantasy. Instead he advocates ways and means which will strengthen the defences, and targets become so hard to attack that the terrorist is soon discouraged. Intelligence efforts such as the infiltration of the terrorist group to learn of their plans, tactics and personalities (particularly the leadership) is a long-term patient strategy which can pay handsome dividends. Armed with such information, the authorities can wage an effective propaganda war by exploiting rivalries and undermining cohesion. Inducements to terrorists, if properly handled, can be very effective. The Italians broke the back of the Red Brigades and other assorted groups through its system of *penitos*, whereby terrorists who co-operated when they were captured received more lenient treatment and prison sentences. The British experience of plea bargaining through the 'supergrass' method has in contrast proved singularly unsuccessful in Northern Ireland.

The terrorists, too, are aware of these devices. Their organisation these days is more tightly knit and professionally structured to make it that much harder for the authorities to penetrate. They can always count on the lethargy of the authorities to promote and sustain a high degree of vigilance. If the target is a Pan-Am flight, it matters little if the security at Heathrow is too tight, for Karachi will suffice.

Terrorists often live in fear of the group, more than they fear the military. They have lost the idea of the importance of life and deviance from the group can result in swift retribution, kneecapping and often death. There is constant emphasis, too, on the potency of the tools of the trade. Many survivors of terrorist kidnaps have commented in their debriefs on how terrorists caress their weapons, often in a sexually explicit but subconscious fashion.

We are all to a large degree products of our environment. One of the most disturbing trends in contemporary terrorism is that we are now into the era of the 'third generation'. Many young people living in the trouble spots of the world such as Northern Ireland, the Middle East, Central and Latin America and now Southern Africa, know only a world where terrorism is a fact of life. Children of the streets in Belfast or Beirut know only a world encompassed by patrolling troops and militia, riots, bombings and the sniper. They are conditioned by acts of violence.

The experts talk of primary socialisation, those formative years up to the age of about five, in which so much human behaviour is shaped by experience. This childhood experience of terrorism has produced a third generation terrorist who is more ruthless than ever, and the spiral of violence escalates as such people move into positions of leadership within the group. The terrorist of the twenty-first century is already alive and experiencing those formative influences that will alienate him from society and propel him along the path of violence.

6 Terrorist Profiles

What sort of people become terrorists? Many theses have been written on the subject and none have or ever will produce a satisfactory answer. Certain commonalities will be found and analysed but they are not of a substance of any use to those contemplating counterterrorist measures or simply trying to harden themselves as targets. The subject is plainly impossible to quantify. For every thesis there is a counter thesis. Why is it that a large part of a country's population can have a very real and indisputable grievance and yet this does not produce terrorism; and yet a very small and insignificant grievance will produce a major terrorist movement? The balance between the use of terrorism by extreme left-wing political groups and extreme right-wing groups is probably fairly even. In fact, go East to the Middle East and beyond; go West to South America and beyond and the left-wing right-wing terminology loses all meaning.

Hardly ever, if the digging is deep enough, will there be found a true 'revolutionary socialist' base to the inspirations of a terrorist group. The rhetoric of Marx, Castro, Guevara may well be used but the true motivations will usually lie within religion, nationalism, racialism and extremism. The oft-quoted co-operation between groups is misleading, more often than not the collusion is between individuals and not groups.

We can see this in the Irish situation. The IRA is amongst the oldest of the terrorist groups and it is so totally different from the PFLP, the Red Army Faction, the Red Brigade, the Japanese Red Army *et al*. that it might be a class alone. Nationalism, sentimentalism and patriotism are all motivations which have impact upon the Irish character; to many it is a game. Outsiders are treated with suspicion, the tactics of the international terrorist groups are treated with contempt. The only assistance which is warmly welcomed is from the Irish-American community which is a link formed on misplaced and misunderstood sympathy and sheer sentimentalism. The loss of this aid, if it continues to dry up at the currently progressive rate, may well force the IRA to turn to other hands to feed them but it will be a gesture based on necessity and not a common cause.

The IRA gives the lie to many stated characteristics of the terrorist. It is not composed purely of young bloods. The very fact that the cause is historical attracts many mature men and (a minority) women. Although the leaders may be both intellectual and eloquent, the majority of the members are less so and come from working-class backgrounds. The principal aims of the movement have been deliberately kept simple – Boot the British (and the Army) out of Northern Ireland – and they have appeal. There is no high-flown political fol-de-rol, no Marxist revolutionary phrases to learn. The real aim of the IRA may be much more than the removal of the British but nonetheless that is their recruiting banner cry.

There is a similarity of purpose with the organisations making up the Palestinian Liberation Forces, in that they are also involved in a pure territorial conflict with the Jews. Circumstances have made the Palestinians turn to procuring assistance from other international groups. Whilst an Irishman may not look like an Irishman, an Arab does look like an Arab. With the eyes of the security forces of the world looking for Arabs in particular threat areas and situations, they have been forced to seek this external aid. This has led to joint operations with the Baader-Meinhof, the Red Army Faction the Japanese Red Army and of course the Sanchez (Carlos) connection of many years standing.

Is there then a typical terrorist? Probably not, but there is perhaps some similarity of breeding and recruiting ground. The society in which terrorism occurs is generally speaking either a Parliamentary democracy or an authoritarian regime, usually a badly run one at that. It will not be found in the totalitarian society; where is the point? If the actions are not going to receive any publicity or public debate, there is no way to put this message before the world and without this the cause is lost before it starts.

Within these societies the recruiting targets are likely to be found among the frustrated and jobless; the young, idle rich; and the criminal element. The common bond initially seems to be the excitement of 'doing something' against the 'system'; there is an element of sexuality and drug taking – the lure of the commune style of living with its free sexual experimentation and the mutual congratulations for the ideology which they discuss among themselves. It is all an enticement in the early stages of recruitment.

The real dedication is only apparent amongst the leaders and they generally set themselves apart from the rest as much in the interests of their security as anything else. Alert to the fact that motivations are not necessarily the same or as intense as his own the leader will invariably allow his followers to fuel themselves on their own rhetoric without trying to impose his own views on them. The leader will usually be the planner and only take assistance in the form of technical expertise i.e. bomb design and manufacture and other such allied necessities.

It is difficult to be confidently accurate about the profiles of terrorists still in the business. They are on the whole very secure, the boasts they make cannot be believed as they usually contain an element of red herrings. Police files are necessarily guarded and journalists are reluctant to indicate their sources. This is particularly so in the case of the IRA where internal discipline is the harshest of all terrorist groups. Death for informers, 'kneecappings' (being shot in the back of the knee), the crude amputation of fingers and even castration are punishments meted out for a number of crimes from theft to security leaks of one form or another.

'I am Carlos. You have heard of me. Tell the world.' These or similar words were spoken by 'Carlos' on the occasion of the kidnapping of eleven OPEC ministers in Vienna in December 1975. Indeed most of the world had probably heard of 'Carlos' by that time. Man of mystery, the elusive pimpernel of the terrorist world and reputed to be the character base for Frederick Forsyth's *The Day of the Jackal*. What sort of man is 'Carlos' and where did he start on his trail of terror?

He is probably the most discussed individual terrorist figure in the media today. There is a wealth of conflicting material but the common threads supported by police files show that 'Carlos', or Ilich Ramirez Sanchez, as he was born, had an extremely fortunate start in life. Born in October 1949 to Jose Allagracia Sanchez and his wife Elba, in Caracas, Venezuela, Ilich was immediately surrounded by wealth. More than wealth, he was born into a revolutionary family (his name is one of Stalin's); his grandfather was active in the 1899 Revolution and his father was a staunch, highly opinionated Stalinist. He grew up in luxury, his father being a lawyer turned property magnate and a millionaire. Little is known about the young Ilich except that he progressed through communist student organisations, a training session in Cuba and somewhere between 1968 and 1971 he attended the Lumumba University in Moscow. It is during this time that he is believed to have made his first contacts with the Palestinians with whom he has worked so closely ever since.

He was certainly in the ranks of the PFLP at the time of the Dawson's Field incident and in the struggle to resist King Hussein of

Jordan's operation which finally ejected the group from the country. It is said that it was during this period that he made his impact on the PFLP and in particular Wadi Haddad. 1972 found him in London and with his mother on the diplomatic social network. Money was apparently no object and probably still came from his father. It is during this year that he first appears on the Special Branch 'watch list'. Although they were not to be attributed to him for some years, Ilich is now known to have carried out two attacks in London during his time in the city, the attempt on the life of Lord Sieff, president of Marks and Spencer in December 1973 and, in February 1974, the bomb attack on the Israeli Hapoalim Bank.

From London he moved to Paris where he conducted operations on behalf of the PFLP and also assisted the Japanese Red Army in a bombing attack. The French became aware of Ilich's operations by chance when they raided the apartment of a man they had under observation purely on suspicion. A subsequent interrogation led them to corner Ilich in another apartment but, with great coolness and presence of mind, he shot his way out of the cordon. In December 1975 the operation in which the eleven OPEC ministers were taken hostage was carried out. One of Ilich's five comrades was seriously wounded in the action and later gave much valuable information about him. The OPEC affair was settled with a large ransom paid by Saudi Arabia and Iran. It has been conjectured that Colonel Qaddafi had an inspirational input to the operation.

Ilich was certainly involved in masterminding the Air France hijack which ended so conclusively in Entebbe in June 1976. A few months after this incident Ilich appeared on the scene in Libya in the principal role as trainer. Presumably he was so well documented on the files of the international security agencies that it was not considered safe for him to operate in person, at least for a while. From Libya he went to work in Syria and on behalf of that country moved back into Europe to mount operations against the dissident Moslems in Paris. During a prelude to one of these operations, two members of Ilich's old revolutionary cells were captured and the hunt was on again. The two comrades were jailed and Ilich wrote to the French Embassy in the Hague threatening action against the French government if they were not released. Around the area of the deadline given in the letter there were two bomb attacks in Paris both of which could have been attributed to Ilich but the French government stood firm. The prisoners served their sentences and on their release, one of them, a German, Magdalena Kaupp, married Ilich.

Is 'Carlos' now retired? It is extremely unlikely, for apart from the obvious enjoyment of the game, he has a constant need for money to support his extravagant lifestyle. He is well known to the authorities in Europe who probably have his location; he has made enemies in the Middle East, particularly in Libya, but despite this it is likely to be in conjunction with a Middle Eastern cause that he will appear again. That Ilich had no financial reason to turn to a career in terror is certain. It is not easy to pin an ideological motivation on him but his enjoyment of the life, its excitement and the glamour of the 'Great Carlos' image obviously fill a need in him. His extreme arrogance in personally signing the threat to the French government would appear to be entirely in keeping with his character insofar as it is known and he has earned a grudging respect in some quarters for his organising ability and undoubted courage. Whatever his motives, whatever his character, 'Carlos' certainly stands out as a truly international figure.

Another inspired terrorist leader who came from wealthy beginnings is Abu Nidal. Born Sabri al Banna into a rich trading family he became the head of one of the most feared of the Middle East terrorist organisations. Abu Nidal (The Father of the Struggle) shared many of Carlos' traits: supreme arrogance – when, after the shooting of Shlomo Argov (Israeli Ambassador) in June 1982, his three-man hit team was arrested and subsequently sentenced to 30 years in jail, Abu Nidal made the statement, '. . . the zionist British judges will learn about justice . . .'. The killings of Kenneth Whitty, First Secretary at the British Embassy in Athens in March 1984 and of Percy Norris, British Deputy High Commissioner in Bombay in November 1984 are both ascribed to Abu Nidal. Abu Nidal is a far more secretive man than Carlos and was himself on the death list of other terrorist organisations. It was generally believed for a time that he died of a heart attack in late 1984 but there was no concrete evidence of this and a temporary disappearance from the operational scene would surely have been a sensible thing for him. There is little doubt that he is active once more.

Ulrike Meinhof's background was secure and affluent. With her husband Klaus Rainer Rohl, she lived well. She was a fêted journalist on his left-wing magazine, *Konkret*, which had a political content. It was on the dissolution of their marriage that she appears to have joined the much younger student 'commune set' and received her first exposure to student politics. This life brought her into close personal contact with Gudrun Ensslin, at that time the lover of Andreas Baader, dissolute braggart and student failure who had been attracted to the easy life of the revolutionary. Their philosophies, real on the part of Ensslin and largely imagined by Baader, caught her attention as the group became more active. When Baader was arrested, it took little persuading for her to assist Ensslin actively in effecting the jail break-in to rescue him. That was her entry into the pages of the history books which was to end in October 1977 with her suicide in Stuttgart's Stammheim prison.

The world has produced a large number of very determined women terrorists all of whom have achieved either positions of leadership or notoriety. The spread is international. Ulrike Meinhof and Gudrun Ensslin (B-M, RAF); Nancy Perry and Patty Hearst (SLA); Fusako Shigenobo (JRA); Angelika Speitel (Croissant Group); Leila Khaled (PFLP); are but a few who spring readily to mind. Psychiatrists put the proliferation in numbers of women terrorists down to a need to liberate themselves through violence and prove their superiority over men. The truth of the matter is debatable but generally women terrorists are demonstrably much more callous and cruel than their male counterparts.

To be successful in the terrorist trade requires all the attributes normally sought in the good military officer. A high degree of leadership in getting the best performance from his followers who may not share his dedication. Sound planning and organisational ability are essential. The ability to attract and manage finance is vital as the cut out security system demands a lot of personal responsibility in this area. Total dedication to the cause but that cause may have a wide base as in the case of Carlos (to inspire and maintain world revolution). Most useful of all is to be able to tie in the planning ability to a sound understanding of the news media and the effect it can have on the public, for this is the means by which the greatest influence is attracted.

7 Terrorist Targets

'Embassy bombed!'
'Aircraft hijacked!'
'Public house blasted!'
'Oranges poisoned!'
'Ambassador assassinated!'
'Businessman kidnapped!'
'Racehorse stolen!'
'Right-wing politician in sex scandal!'

Not literally transcribed admittedly, but all the incidents above have made headlines in the last decade. The motives were different but all the events had at least two things in common; they were terrorist inspired and they were grist for the media mill. What is a terrorist target? An almost impossible question. It is anyone or anything which can be attacked in a dramatic manner and tied to the terrorist cause no matter however loosely, with the aim of frightening the majority. It is important to the international traveller, not because he is necessarily a target, but because he may often be in the company of a target; be housed with one; be travelling in one, or merely be the object which is in the way.

If we confine ourselves initially to using the word 'target' without further definition it will help to show, by incident, why some particular targets have been chosen. The kidnap and subsequent murder of Hans Martin Schleyer in September 1977 satisfied a number of target selection factors. The outrage drew worldwide attention once more to the Baader-Meinhof group and the Red Army Faction; it was revenge against the deaths of their comrades in Stuttgart prison and the assault on the Lufthansa aircraft at Mogadishu, and it severely disrupted the West German government, still reeling from the earlier murders of Buback and Pontoe, prominent members of the business community. The bomb at Orly airport in July 1983 was used, no doubt, by the Armenian Secret Army for the Liberation of Armenia, to remind the world that they are still around. The drawing of attention to the 'cause' is a factor but the target need have no actual connection to that cause!

Even now, five years later, the motives behind the assassination attempt on Pope John Paul II by Mehmet Ali Agca remain a mystery. Agca was a known assassin on the Interpol files, a member of the Turkish Gray Wolves. Theories have been propounded that Agca was working under instructions from the Bulgarian Secret Service. If so – why? For a trained assassin to make such a clumsy attempt knowing that his chances of escape were minimal suggests that for some strange reason he 'threw the rule book away'.

Forget for the moment any rhetoric or dissertation on terrorist ideals and philosophies. Let us look at what they actually do and their basic methods of operation. Of concern to the reader are those actions which could spin off and affect them in day to day business life and travel:

'Street' murder: the shooting and killing of innocent people in public places, e.g. the Abu Nidal attacks on El Al airport check-in desks in Rome and Vienna in December 1985.

'Street' bombing: the bombing of public places and killing of innocents, e.g. the Provisional IRA (PIRA) bomb attacks on Harrods of London in December 1983.

Aircraft hijack: the siezing of control of an aircraft regardless of the passenger manifest to negotiate the release of terrorist prisoners, e.g. the Islamic Jihad hijack of the Air France 737 en route from Frankfurt to Paris, July 1984.

Aircraft mid-air bombing: e.g. the Air India 747 en route from Toronto to London exploded in mid-air off the Irish coast in June 1985. Believed to be the work of Sikh Extremists.

Assassination of political figures: often when bombs are used it results in innocents also being killed, e.g. the attempt on General Grivas in the BEA Comet, October 1967.

Seizure of buildings: the seizure of embassies or corporate buildings with innocent people becoming hostages, e.g. the Iranian Embassy siege in London, May 1980.

The above is a fairly random selection of typical terrorist operations which through their nature can prove a threat to the innocent traveller or bystander. When the list is extended to include the train hijack in Holland by the South Moluccans and the seizure of the Italian cruise liner *Achille Lauro* in the Mediterranean in October 1985 it puts into perspective the travelling risk created by terrorism. Kidnapping is one aspect of terrorism which is worth considering at this stage. It has been the subject of numerous books, though many aspects of it seem to be a closed chapter, perhaps due to the

influence of the insurance underwriters. This threat remains high on
the list of individual concerns.

There have been some notable accounts of kidnapping and at the
top of any executive reading list should be Sir Geoffrey Jackson's
story of his ordeal at the hands of the Tupamaros.[1] (Not to be
confused with the Tupac Amaros of Peru.) At the time of his
abduction, Sir Geoffrey was the British Ambassador in Uruguay.
He had known from his own observations that he was a potential
candidate for kidnap by the Tupamaros. Early 1970 saw a spate of
political kidnappings in the continent cutting across a wide spectrum
of nationalities: Russian, West German, American, Japanese and
Guatemalan.

So sure was Jackson that he had been targeted that he liaised with
the Foreign Office in London to agree the mutual stance that would
be adopted in the event. The kidnap took place on 8 January 1971.
The Ambassador's car was ambushed by a group of armed terrorists
and though no shots were fired, Jackson was beaten up. The stance
taken by him and the Foreign Office had been agreed on that visit to
London six months earlier; there would be no bending before any
pressure no matter what threats were made. For some eight months
Jackson maintained his dignity despite being housed in vile
conditions. Further, as his book shows, he used his time to study the
backgrounds and motives of those who held him captive, and the
book gives some startling insights into the Tupamaros as well as
being perhaps a classic documentation on retaining personal values
under stress.

Jackson was of course a political kidnap victim and this particular
act is perhaps where the terrorists become the closest to being
assessed as common criminals. Whether it is a criminal or political
case, the tactics are virtually the same. At the end of the day both
parties, the government and the terrorist gang, each have a
'commodity' which the other party wants. Political kidnaps often
have as their 'ransom' the freedom of imprisoned comrades;
criminals on the other hand are usually seeking large amounts of
untraceable cash. It is interesting to note that in some kidnap
'centres', and Italy is a prime example, it is not at all uncommon for
terrorists to rent criminal expertise in effecting the abduction.
Certainly the Red Brigade has in the past utilised the talents of a
Calabrian gang on more than one occasion and in one particular
case the negotiating 'fingerprint' suggests that the gang also
supervised the bargaining process.

In the past it would have been fair to say that the kidnappings in Italy were largely criminal acts for hard cash; in the other prime area of Latin America a large percentage were politicians. The year 1986–7, however, is showing a changing trend. After a worldwide decline in the crime in 1984 and 1985, it seems to be on the increase again. It is difficult to quote the figures, since generally every attempt is made by families and insurance brokers to keep quiet about the events for many sound reasons. In many countries it is illegal to pay ransoms, though some of these countries have legal bodies willing to turn a 'blind eye' if it is in the victim's interests.

In the USA perhaps the most realistic attitude is adopted by the FBI. They are willing to resist the temptation to locate and assault the gang's hideout and will content themselves with trying to monitor the handover of cash and hope to deal with the gang after the victim is released. It is a sensible approach and one which virtually assures them of the co-operation of the family in passing on all available information which, in the last analysis, will help both the FBI in trapping the gang and the courts of law when they are brought to trial.

In Italy it is illegal to pay a ransom, but many families are suspicious of the ability of the police to handle rescues. This is perhaps a little unfair, but nonetheless the feeling exists – it is also exacerbated by a fear of declaring true wealth because of the danger of exposing a non-payment of taxes. An anomaly which eases the Italian situation a little, however, is the law which in effect states that 'a law can be broken if the intention is to save life' – a phlegmatic and workable solution.

Over the last 18 months, case study availability has shown an increase in kidnapping in Peru, Columbia and Guatemala, with a recurrence in Italy. The reasons will be many and varied but in the South American countries one school of thought is that where it used to be very easy for small criminals to make a reasonable living from narcotics trading, it has now become such a well-organised business that the major syndicates have squeezed out those small-time operators whom they do not wish to use. Hence kidnapping has begun to flourish again. Kidnapping is not necessarily targeted against the known rich. In Peru and Colombia unpremeditated kidnaps have occurred simply because the victim appeared to have money because of the way he/she dressed or the shops he/she visited.

Executives in wealthy corporations have always been at risk and there is every indication that this will increase. Large corporate bodies now take out insurance policies. This does not decrease the risk (indeed some people think it may increase it) but it does defray costs and can give the corporate headquarters access to a skilled consultant to advise on negotiation tactics.

A story well known in consultant circles demonstrates probably the fastest negotiation on record. An Italian father was contacted by a gang who informed him that his youngest daughter had been abducted that afternoon. A ransom was demanded if he wished ever to see her alive again. The Italian's reply was along the following lines: 'I have ten children, they are all a trial and annoyance to me. They are expensive to keep and took only a few seconds to conceive. One less is not a problem – it's a help.' With that he is reputed to have put the phone down. The gang was convinced and the daughter was immediately released. Not an advised course of action if the executive work force is to feel secure!

Kidnaps will continue and prevention for the executive or diplomat is formidably difficult in the physical sense. It requires large numbers of well-trained car teams with good communications and is extremely expensive to maintain. Embassy or corporate life and business would suffer in the extreme if the 'fortress' option were to be applied, in which a canton within walls policy is adopted with all the workers travelling to and from work in a protected convoy. This could indeed provoke a stand-off ambush if the terrorists felt sufficiently strongly about the target. The best protection which is affordable perhaps lies in the education of the executives and their families in the simple precautions which help to harden them as targets – they must begin by adopting a clinically selfish attitude. 'If I make myself a difficult target the terrorist will go for someone else. Let the Devil take the hindmost.'

Let us now look at the most highly publicised area of terrorist operation which affects the travelling executive, air travel. It is arguably the most successful venture that terrorists have engaged in so far. Why is it popular? And why does it raise so many emotions? Passenger manifests are usually multinational, have a fair proportion of women and children; communications are good, international airports are usually well within speedy reach of the media cameramen and reporters, and last, but by no means least, the terrorists are already aboard the vehicle which provides them with a sporting chance of a passage to sanctuary and safety. A further consideration is that even with the best trained troops in the world, the grounded aircraft presents the most difficult target to assault, especially now that terrorists have learned some of the lessons of Mogadishu and similar incidents. It is far less the actual hijack but more the prevention of such that will interest the reader. After all, once he has been hijacked, the traveller can literally only obey the basic rules of non-aggressive eye contact or movement, stay low profile and 'go along for the ride', hoping for a safe conclusion to his flight.

In the last ten years security at airports has been the most contentious aspect of travel. A vast amount of money has been spent on the problem, yet explosives and weapons are still smuggled aboard with remarkable regularity. Why is this and what, if anything, is being done to stop it? The first consideration is that air travel has had the effect of shrinking the world and by-passing frontiers. Business which used to be days distant is now only hours away and the entrepreneurial instincts of man make him eager to use the transport despite the risk. Risk versus return has always been one of the most difficult business calculables.

World tourism is at a peak, bringing in millions of international pleasure-seekers to the airports; never was it more true to say 'the sky's the limit'. Take away the risk factor and air travel is popular because it is generally efficient, affordable, pleasant and easy. The factors inherent to any improvements to air travel security measures are essentially commercial and humane. Although the commercial factor is placed first and is indeed the final arbiter, it is two aspects of the human factor which force commerce into this position.

For every twenty consultants who say 'there is no such thing as total security', will be found eighty who will disagree. Granted, the latter may qualify their claim with remarks about the downgraded and possibly unacceptable quality of life. Sadly the twenty are correct. There is no absolute copyright on ingenuity – whatever one man can put together, somewhere there will be a man with the ability to take it apart. This is highly relevant to the technical aids to security at airports. Not only this but the second human factor of frailty comes in. It can be considered in three forms: greed, the ability to concentrate and shortness of memory. Start with the last factor: the short memory. In the immediate aftermath of a highly-publicised terrorist hijack there is a public outcry over how the weapons or explosives got aboard. 'Tighten up security', the public scream, and for a short time they accept the long queues at security search counters, nodding wisely to each other and murmuring platitudes. Within weeks they are shouting about delay, inefficiency and the like. The newspapers are full of other items; the hijack is long forgotten. Short memory syndrome, like 'Sod's Law', has struck again.

On the whole, technical aids such as the X-ray baggage inspection system and explosives detectors are efficient. They will do their job through a two-, four-, six- or eight-hour shift, inspecting bag after bag and box after box. Sadly the human attention span to a black and white monitor image, no matter how good the quality, is severely limited. So limited in fact that the interval before a mesmeric effect takes over is measured in minutes not hours. Not even the most physically fit or well motivated person can be relied on to interpret the shades, patterns and lines of ever-moving luggage on the small monitor accurately. Test yourself with your home TV; how long can you concentrate totally without moving your eyes from the screen? Psychologists would maintain that efficiency in performance and the attention span drops away rapidly after 12–15 minutes. Many airport authorities are proud to proclaim that they rotate their security crews every 45 minutes; in some locations they simply move them to another monitor!

Commercially of course airlines and airports just could not cope with the congestion, delays and flight cancellations which would result from properly searching all passengers.

It has often been suggested that a total sterilisation of airports would greatly assist in preventing the bomber. In this context sterilisation means a complete exclusion of non-travellers from within the outer perimeter. No friends and family with whom to have a farewell coffee, no spectator arenas, nothing but the previously ticketed and computer checked traveller with all queueing taking place at the outer perimeter. Inside, nothing at all – no coffee shops, news stands – nothing. The financial losses would be enormous to the satellite businesses, airport taxes and rentals would increase and this would be passed on to the public who would protest bitterly at the higher cost of tickets.

What can be done? Public education to show the traveller what to look out for, and encourage him to report it, would help. Would the increase in adrenalin flow be sufficient to increase the efficiency of searchers if they were to travel on the aircraft with the passengers and baggage they are inspecting? Would it be possible for each flight to carry its own inspection crew? It would certainly be an upgrading of incentive. There is little the traveller can do at international airports except to stay alert and minimise the amount of time he spends lounging around in close proximity to threatened check-in desks. Arrive early, get through the formalities of check in, searching and immigration and spend the waiting time in the safest area, the immediate departure lounge.

The skymarshal was deployed by the FBI and Israeli security forces at roughly the same time. He was armed and strategically placed in the aircraft, but sadly he was a fairly impotent feature of in-flight security, and indeed probably more of a liability under some circumstances. Nevertheless for a long time the publicity surrounding his presence was enough to reduce the threat considerably.

The protection of corporate headquarters is far easier. Control of visitors properly logged and checked against pre-recorded appointments is largely sufficient if it is backed up by proper security awareness programmes for all staff (see Chapter 17). Hotels can pose a problem – they have been terrorist targets for many years – but any corporate headquarters nowadays should be able to provide its mobile executives with a basic threat assessment in respect of international venues. It is not difficult to establish through commercial attachés, the ownership and affiliations of good class hotels and then it is a matter of being guided by the threat assessment.

Although kidnapping and air travel present the major risks to the diplomat and executive, it should not be forgotten that other forms of abduction have taken place in an effort to extort money from corporations and private individuals. The theft of Shergar in County Kildare, Southern Ireland, occupied as much news space in the United Kingdom as an aircraft hijack would have done. This highly prized racehorse, winner of the Derby and the apple of the Aga Khan's eye, was taken from its stable in February 1983. A ransom was demanded but negotiations, being handled by a private company, broke down and it is generally supposed that the horse is now dead. The Provisional IRA (PIRA) is attributed with responsibility.

There would not appear to be a statistical basis upon which to calculate peak terrorist action times but many do appear on anniversaries of so-called martyrs and during religious festival periods. The PIRA have certainly targeted the United Kingdom during the Christmas period for a number of years. Again, a national threat assessment should include such potentially violent periods if they exist.

It would be morally wrong to discuss in detail the potential targets open to the terrorist groups which they have so far ignored. Suffice it to say that there are a number of sites where the effects of a terrorist attack would be catastrophic.

NOTE

1. Sir Geoffrey Jackson, *People's Prison* (London: Faber, 1973).

8 Assassination

'. . . is the extreme form of censorship'
George Bernard Shaw, *The Rejected Statement*, Part 1

It is sad but only sensible to reflect that the breakdown in traditional standards with the increasing willingness to use violence to achieve political ends has produced terrorist organisations in virtually all countries. The word 'assassination' itself has an interesting derivation. It sprang from the early Crusades to the Holy Wars in the Middle East when a tactic used by the great Islamic leader, Saladin, had a profound effect on morale and efficiency. He administered hashish to his 'night warriors'; drugged and full of religious fervour they would infiltrate the tent lines of the Crusaders by dark and cut the throats of the sleeping soldiers. These men became known by the Arab term 'hashish'een' and from this came the word as we know it today. So, the assassin has been with us for centuries but his art has become much more refined through the ages.

Pause to reflect on some of the world leaders who have been assassinated in recent years and note the geographical spread: President Allende (Chile); President Shermarke (Somalia); President Mondlane (Mozambique); President Bandaranaike (Sri Lanka); Kings Saud and Faisal (Saudi Arabia); President Remon (Panama); Tom M'boya (Kenya); Sir Richard Sharples (Governor of Bermuda); Sheikh Othman (North Yemen); President Ratisimandrava (Malagasy); Sheikh Rahman (Bangladesh); President Tombalbaye (Chad); President Kennedy (USA); President Mohammed (Nigeria); Airey Neave (England); President Anwar Sadat (Egypt); Mrs Indira Gandhi (India). There have even been attempts on the life of the Pope and on Mrs Thatcher. The list, if it were given in full and also included the hundreds of unsuccessful attempts, would be extensive and frightening in its global coverage.

The last twenty years have seen successful coups d'état in approximately 60 per cent of African countries. Eighteen of the twenty-two countries of Latin America have experienced successful coups, with attempts in four others; while sixty-two per cent of Asian countries have suffered similar fates, with attempts in most of the others. Although coups d'état are not so prevalent in the Middle

73

East (only about 50 per cent), assassinations and attempted assassinations of political and traditional leaders are quite common.

If violence is successfully used as the means to a political end, it can become almost endemic. One figure after another, having been shown the route, will force his way to the front for what he feels is his rightful period of tenure in power; so, it will be seen that coups and assassinations rarely protect a country from the spread of further violence. Take Argentina as an example: just between 1951 and 1953 it experienced eight coups. It has had at least as many since then and is little nearer to stability. It can be fairly safely predicted that the increasing sophistication of weapons and transport, and a broadening of motivation caused by a world full of complex political questions and moral dilemmas, for which there are few answers, will lead to violent changes of government becoming more and more common.

Assassination is one of the occupational hazards of all political leaders, it always has been and probably always will be, but how does it affect the business traveller? It concerns him in a number of ways; knowledge of the techniques, the motivations and the aims of the assassin are part of the overall understanding of terrorism. More and more business ventures, particularly in Second and Third World countries, are subject to discussion and negotiation in very high political arenas, often at President and Vice-President level. In many cases this state of affairs has been brought about by terrorism in itself. Corrupt leaders or leaders determined to stamp out corruption often owe their positions to self-engineered, successful coups d'état. Once in power they are reluctant to delegate financial control to others. Whether the motivation is lack of trust or a desire to swell their own 'contingency fund' is almost by-the-by to the business executive, but it does mean that from time to time he may find himself in close proximity to a terrorist or political target. The machine gun and especially the bomb do not discriminate; just to be on the scene, no matter how innocently, may lead to incarceration by security forces in a hostile country.

It is interesting and important (in the later context of the book) to look at the assassin's main motivation. Individual motivations are very complex and not easy to explain. Often the assassin is killed in the attempt; often it is difficult to get information from him even if he is captured; frequently terrorist groups will take advantage of an unplanned assassination to claim responsibility for their own publicity reasons. In some notable cases, the truth is never satisfactorily revealed; look at the myth, rumour and subterfuge which still continues to surround the assassination of J. F. Kennedy. Generally speaking, the motivations will fall into one or a combination of the following categories:

political
religious
criminal
financial
psychopathic
racial

The outcome of an assassination very often bears no resemblance to the original aims of the killer. This is particularly the case if the target is a Head of State or holds another such high political office. Probably one of the best examples of this is the assassination on 28 June 1914 of Archduke Franz Ferdinand of Austria. Six assassins were involved and it is still debated in historical circles whether General Potiorek, who was travelling with Franz Ferdinand at the time, was the true target. Regardless of the eventual outcome of this debate it is certain that the anarchist group, the Black Hand Society, who plotted the assassination, had something far less in mind than the violence and savagery unleashed by the First World War which immediately followed the Sarajevo incident.

Many everyday objects can be turned into weapons; the range of devices is limited only by man's ingenuity and the operational needs of the time. The weapons selected in a 'kill to order' operation are usually governed by one of two important requirements: does the killer intend to escape after the 'hit'? Does the weapon need to be concealed to get it to the point of action?

With the exception of the deliberate 'martyr', and he is normally confined to the Middle East and often has a religious inspiration, the modern-day terrorist generally wishes to make good his escape after the operation. This has resulted in the popularity of the remotely-controlled explosive device followed closely by the long-range firearm. The use of the remotely controlled system is not as new as is generally thought. Consider the following extract:

. . . Bound for Armed Forces Day ceremonies at Caracas Military School, Venezuelan President Romulo Betancourt rode through the city streets in the presidential limousine chatting with Defence Minister José Lopez Henriquez and Mrs. Henriquez, who were beside him. . . . Chauffeur Azael Valero swung the black presidential car onto the Avenida de los Proceros . . . ahead on the divided street sat a parked 1945 Oldsmobile. . . .

Suddenly, the Oldsmobile disintegrated into a thousand shreds of shrapnel, a blinding ball of flame, and a column of smoke 1000 feet tall. Betancourt's car was hurled onto the centre grass strip and burst into flames. The President and his Minister managed to push open the left rear door and pull Mrs. Henriquez to safety. Badly burned, Chauffeur Valero and a presidential aide, Colonel Ramon Armas Perez, tumbled out of the front seat. . . .[1]

In fact Betancourt survived the attempt, but Perez was not so lucky – he died shortly after arrival at the hospital.

Up until about ten years ago, the pistol was by far the most popular assassination weapon; probably due to the ease of concealment and acquisition. The drawback with the pistol, however, is the need to get close to the target and a very high percentage of the killers using the weapon have subsequently been apprehended. It is interesting to note that a large number of the pistol-wielding assassins who have been arrested have been or have claimed to be suffering from mental disorders. Whether this is a statement of reality and they actually were so afflicted, or whether they had been cleverly chosen by the organisations who funded the killings, or whether they were simply using very plausible 'cover stories' will never be known. Politicians in the USA in particular seem to have suffered at the hands of the psychopath. Just to take the last twenty years, two of the Kennedy brothers suffered at the hands of such men; Governor Wallace of Alabama was crippled by a so-called lunatic; Martin Luther King was gunned down; and in Japan 1969, US Secretary of State Rodgers and the American Ambassador Richard Meyer were attacked by Shiget Sugu Hamaoko, a knife-wielding psychopath.

Bizarre weapons have featured throughout time. Leon Trotsky, a leader of the 1917 Bolshevik Revolution and first Commissar of the Red Army, exiled by Stalin on 30 August 1940, was murdered in Mexico. The weapon of choice for Ramon Mercader was a mountaineer's ice axe. On 2 January 1969, Emperor Hirohito of Japan was standing on the balcony of the royal palace, waving to a crowd of approximately 14,000 persons, during his annual New Year's Day appearance. His attacker, Kenzo Okuzaki, fired four steel pachinko balls at the Emperor using a slingshot. As Okuzaki was standing at ground level at a considerable distance from the Emperor, he narrowly missed. It should be noted that Okuzaki was already on a police watch list as a dangerous person (as indeed was Lee Harvey Oswald, J. F. Kennedy's supposed killer) and it illustrates the point that such people should perhaps be put into preventive detention during major public appearances by VIPs under threat. Perhaps the truest return to the 'hashish'een' is epitomised by Tidiano Keita when he ran from the crowd and tried to strangle President Sek Toure of Guinea. Keita was later found to have been smoking 'chanvre', an opium type drug.

The introduction of poison into the human system is probably the oldest method of assassination known. It certainly is one of the most effective methods for allowing the assassin to remain undetected. At the same time it is not strictly necessary, with the possible exceptions of the financial and psychopath motives, to kill if the desired result is the removal of the target from effective office. If this can be achieved against a Head of State or senior politician by a means which will discredit the individual, his politics and his party, so much the better. Obviously, then, if a professional assassin can induce brain damage, blindness or cancers of the liver, bladder and kidneys, he has achieved his objective. The long terminal illness of the victim can be exploited by use of a smear campaign. What better way to discredit a political movement than its leader should die blind, insane and rotten with syphilis? Horrific? Yes, but the KGB are known to have used Caesium 137 as an assassination method for the last twenty years or more. The victim requires only one meal laced with this innocuous white powder to die of renal cancer within about nine months. The interested reader could set himself an intriguing exercise by researching the number of West European politicians who have died of renal cancer in the last two decades.

The petro-chemical industries of the twentieth century provide easy access to bulk supplies of toxic substances with a strength and chemical complexity which is unprecedented. These substances can be introduced through the lungs, the skin or the stomach and, if carefully chosen, can give symptoms almost indistinguishable from natural causes. This is one of the reasons that the protection of medical records is so vitally important in the security of a VIP. A man prone to heart attacks or any number of other everyday modern illnesses is an easy target, because his symptoms can be mimicked by the skilful application of commonly available toxic substances.

The liquids trichloroethane, trichloroethylene, perchloroethylene and carbon tetrachloride are particularly effective. They are all widely available as industrial solvents. If they are subjected to thermal degradation, oxidisation occurs, which produces phosgene (1gm of carbon tetrachloride produces 275mg of phosgene). None of these liquids has a flash point and can be heated without danger of an explosion. Phosgene is a poisonous gas; it has no smell, colour or vapour. It is easily breathed in and was used in the First World War. The symptoms of phosgene poisoning are similar to those of a heart attack; only a detailed autopsy will reveal the true cause. Any of these liquids could easily be introduced into the oil system of a vehicle. When the vehicle is driven and the oil reaches normal running temperature, phosgene will be produced in the engine sump and could exit through the oil breather cap to enter the passenger compartment through the ventilation system. The driver and passengers could suffer heart attacks and all but the most exhaustive examination of the wreckage would fail to show the root cause. The effects of carbon tetrachloride are greatly enhanced if ingested with alcohol, so that even moderate doses can lead to acute poisoning (whisky, carbon tetrachloride and soda). Ingestion of CTC in this form is almost invariably fatal as a result of massive irreversible liver damage (alcoholic poisoning).[2]

The assassinations which have been mentioned in this chapter have been deliberately chosen either to demonstrate a discussion point or because they are relevant to later chapters, showing where lessons still have not been learned despite the passage of time. Apart from being in close proximity to potential targets in the normal course of business and the general need to understand the risks from assassination, it is unlikely that the travelling businessman will himself be a target for the assassin in the classic sense. There is, however, one aspect of assassination which may well concern him either as an influential individual in his own right or as a representative of a publicly responsible corporation in a competitive or sensitive area of commerce. It is an aspect which is not always obvious, but it is possible to take measures to reduce the effect. We are referring to character assassination.

The intention is often to remove the target from the seat of power, not necessarily by killing him. What better way in the business world of removing competition than to discredit the representative or parent company? Many individuals have in their past a seemingly small and insignificant incident which is totally irrelevant to their current life style, business or character. Think what use could be made of some of those facts in the hands of a skilled manipulator of the media. The harmless marijuana cigarette smoked as a juvenile experiment in college days is transformed to the suspicion of addiction to heavy drugs; the short affair is blown up to indicate a man of wild sexual indulgence; traffic offences become the basis for a long criminal record, and so on.

It is quite possible that Cecil Parkinson lost his seat on the Conservative Cabinet as a result of a deliberate exposure and exaggeration of the facts behind his affair with Miss Keays. It has openly been suggested that the smear campaign brought to bear on John Stalker, Deputy Chief Constable of Greater Manchester, was a deliberate move to stop him getting too close to the facts during an investigation he was conducting in Northern Ireland. It is not difficult to investigate the background of any person in a free society and if that society has also bred a news media system which is hungry for the dramatic, eye-catching headline it is a simple thing indeed to put a deliberate character destruction plan into action.

It is the threat of exposure and the subsequent loss of credibility which has made the well-known KGB tactics of sexual compromise followed by blackmail so outstandingly successful – so successful in fact that the true figures will never be known. This style of blackmail has certainly been used by such terrorist groups as the Irish Republican Army (IRA) as a means of extracting both finance and information – again to an unknown extent. How many times during J. F. Kennedy's term of office did rumours reach the press about his alleged affair with Marilyn Monroe? Harold Wilson, when British Prime Minister, came under scathing attack for his friendship with a businessman accused of tax avoidance. This backfired due to the unpredictability of the British public and the Gannex raincoat became a national joke rather than damaging the politician – yet another time and another country could have seen different outcomes to all these cases. It is a serious threat to the businessman.

NOTES

1. *The Times*, 4 July 1960.
2. Von Oettingen, *On Cirrhosis of the Liver*.

9 Terrorist Weapons

The tremendous pressures released as a result of the chemical reaction present in an explosion create a savage interplay of vacuum and counter-forces. The effect on the human body is horrendous: flesh is literally 'sucked' from the bones; those not central to the core area will find muscle and tissue blistering and bubbling with the intense heat; further afield, flying shards of shrapnel, glass and other debris will cause lesser injuries but there will be blood and stupefying shock. The press photographer's chronicle will display a scene of the utmost devastation and horror. Once again the terrorist has achieved his aim: shock, trauma and international publicity.

If the terrorist aim is as stated, small wonder that the bomb, or – more properly – the explosive device, remains high in the tactical arsenal. Quite apart from the dramatic effect and the innate fear and revulsion shown by most people to things explosive, there are other reasons why such devices are popular. To put this into a perspective we should look at what the requirements of the terrorist are in his various and nefarious activities.

If we take the term 'weaponry' as a blanket cover and accept that differing terrorist operations will produce divergent requirements depending upon the aim, target access and the degree of publicity desired, there will still be a commonality of thinking in the selection of the illegal tools of the trade. Think of it as a shopping list; the purchased, stolen or manufactured item will be governed by a series of factors:

availability
popular calibre (firearms)
ease of concealment
accuracy
simplicity of use
reliability
maximum range for minimum size
degree of noise in action (selected operations only)
stand off capability

It is worth briefly taking each of these factors in turn as they relate to virtually every form of weaponry and at some stage will influence planning in most operational scenarios.

Availability. In many Western countries, licensing for explosives is quite stringently enforced, at least as well as is possible without infringing on the constitutional rights of the citizen to possess arms for protection, sporting or vermin control. Equally, there are many countries where such restrictions are either totally non-existent or so loosely applied that they might as well not exist. In some parts of Arabia, the carrying of a weapon traditionally signifies that the bearer has reached manhood. It is certainly not necessary for the bearer of a weapon or the illegal exporter to pass through manned customs posts in order to deliver his cargo of death into the hands of he who can afford to purchase it.

It is still legally acceptable in some countries where licensing is in force to have weapons and ammunition delivered to the customer through normal mail channels. It is not even necessary in some places either to register or to record the actual delivery other than to inform a probably over-worked police force of the recipient's name and licence number.

In every major city in the world there is a black market in firearms, explosives, ammunition and associated devices. These items can be simply war or campaign souvenirs, or they may have been stolen at source or subsequently and skilfully turned out in well-equipped workshops (any public library contains the information for the skilled enthusiast to make his own devices).

The route to availability often takes in corruption and greed. Government departments are reluctant to unveil statistics of theft and 'manoeuvre losses' but in NATO countries alone it is known that such figures run into many hundreds of weapons per year. An informed source states that between the years 1970 and 1975, the US Army reported that 11 000 weapons were stolen, including Redeye surface-to-air missiles. In 1980, charges were brought against civilians for attempting to sell huge amounts of ammunition to the IRA which was later found to have come from US Marine Corps stocks. A well publicised event in that October saw the arrest by the Irish authorities of the trawler *Marita Ann*, who discovered that the arms she was conveying to the PIRA were in fact stolen US Army rifles. Students of physics will be aware that explosive mixtures can be concocted from seemingly innocuous ingredients purchased from the local chemist and supermarket. If they have any doubts, the not-so-underworld press with pamphlets such as 'Be your own 007' and 'Revenge made easy' will help them on their way.

It is doubtful if there is a weapon, from a portable surface-to-air missile through heavy and light machine-guns down to the smallest pistol, which cannot be acquired provided the funding is available. The black market thrives due to man's frailty; the needs of insurgents, terrorists, criminals and collectors ensures this and will continue to do so.

Popular calibres.   Most easily available weapons tend to be those with a large military and para-military market. Obviously such a large market in the weapon leads to an enormous market in ammunition. As an aside, it also establishes a large spare parts holding, and this is a frequent source of the material required to build a totally unregistered weapon.

Unless it is for a highly specialised task, the weapon chosen by the terrorist will be of a popular calibre (9mm for example) in order to ensure a constant and relatively easy source of continued supply. Commercially available re-loading and priming machines which are quite small and can be carried in hand luggage also assist in this respect.

Ease of concealment.   This does not, as it may appear at first sight, confine its application to handguns. There is an increasing number of 'special to purpose' rigs on the market now: Heckler & Kock MP5K; Beretta, Model 12S; UZI; and a large variety of pistols have been fitted into briefcases and other portable means from which they can be accurately fired. Now the advent of small laser beam projectors can lend pin-point precision to these rigs. Small calibres (.22) coupled to easily manufactured silencers, or more properly suppressors, have produced a security agent's nightmare.

Many weapons can be stripped down into a large number of component parts which can greatly assist the terrorist in getting his tools aboard an aircraft targeted for hijack. An increasing trend is for weapons to be produced with little or no metal parts; though the high density plastics and carbon fibres which are used will not defeat X-ray machinery, they can have pieces of a similar material temporarily glued to them to present an everyday profile to all but the most watchful security guards.

Accuracy.   This is a requirement for the specialist. The terrorist engaged in running battles with the forces of law and order is likely to select weapons for their rate of fire and area coverage. The ambush is probably his main tactic, followed by the lightning raid where he wants noise, firepower and is looking for an almost prophylactic effect.

The assassin bent on making his hit with a sniper attack, however, very definitely wants access to a high degree of accuracy. In this age of precision it is not necessarily the rifle towards which he is drawn. Modern sporting needs have persuaded designers to produce an impressive range of heavier calibre (7.62 mm), small (and therefore concealable), extremely accurate long-range pistols. These are geared to use a range of telescopic sights giving a heretofore undreamed-of capability to the assassin. It must be said that as the general market for such firearms is small, at least outside the USA, they do tend to be more difficult for the terrorist to acquire on the black market.

Within the factor of accuracy, do not ignore the 'bomber'. Whilst generally speaking, terrorist bombs or devices tend to be set as a combination of 'kill whoever is in the way' and 'destroy property' basis there are occasions when a great deal of accuracy is required. On particular targets, this precision is possible, although it is normally to be found in the hands of the skilled saboteur. It is perfectly feasible to project a deadly piece of shrapnel, provided it has at least a crude ballistically viable shape, along an accurate trajectory for a considerable distance. It allows the skilled 'craftsman' an ability to construct quite fiendish booby traps or remotely controlled devices at tactically safe working distances from his intended target.

Simplicity of use. Although in the hands of some experienced terrorists sophisticated weaponry undoubtedly plays its part, there is a general desire for uncomplicated, simple to use systems. The terrorist recruiting pool is wide; in many areas it is drawn from uneducated peasantry, often from among students and occasionally from the idle rich. Generally speaking, this recruitment base throws up a class of person with no inherent feel or experience in any form of weaponry.

Recruits may have to be trained in a hurry; indeed they may have to go into action with barely any training whatsoever and therefore their weapons must be simple to use. Most military small arms tend to be simple, not that this indicates the soldier as being unintelligent – the basis for the simplicity is usually geared towards battlefield replenishment and basic repair work by non-technicians.

Simplicity of use is highly pertinent in the field of home-made explosive devices. But the 'home runs' (or self inflicted injuries) scored in Northern Ireland are often the result of the over-simplification of construction, which can lead to negligence in installing safety devices with the inevitable results.

Reliability. This goes hand in hand with the simplicity factor. Terrorist weapons are often subjected to unskilled and lax maintenance, and they may pass from user to user. Weapons may frequently be stored underground in crude wrappings and for long periods (sometimes under water). This is one of the main reasons, after ease of acquisition, why such hardy old tried and trusted weapons such as the Colt Armalite AR 15 & 16, the Soviet AK 47, the M1 carbine, the Sterling SMG, the Browning 9mm pistol, the UZI, the Garand rifle and the MAC 10 Ingram, despite their vintage, still play such a prominent part in the terrorist armoury. This does not detract from the reliability of modern military weapons, indeed far from it, and perhaps the days are upon us now when the Heckler & Koch, Steyr and Beretta range will be encountered more and more by law enforcement agencies.

Maximum range for minimum size.   This is once more a general requirement for the specialist operator, the sniper, the terrorist who intends to make good his escape after the kill. It is fair to say that the market for high-precision, long-range rifles is somewhat smaller than the handgun. An exception would possibly be the USA with its tremendous opportunities for those who travel the remote areas hunting for big game or travelling alone for sheer pleasure when they carry such weapons for shooting or for protection from large animals.

It should not be forgotten that, though a good telescopic sight will not turn a bad shot into a good one, it will greatly enhance the capability of the meagrely equipped marksman. In Europe the question has recently been asked whether precision sights and other firearms-associated devices should not be a matter of licensing. It is a moot point, but in any event it would not be effective in combating the problem.

Degree of noise in action.   'As a terrorist device, the inventor of the "silent" bomb would make a bloody fortune': this was overheard at an international exhibition which had a large section devoted to arms and munitions. A silent bomb is technically impossible, of course, and it is only mentioned to demonstrate that the degree of noise associated with a weapon can be very important to the terrorist. A loud noise under particular circumstances may be just as desirable as the lack of noise in another scenario, as exemplified by 'Bloody Friday' (21 July 1972) in Belfast, Northern Ireland. This saw the seeding of about twenty devices in the city in the same afternoon set to detonate during peak shopping hours. The noise was to be an important factor in the disorientation and creation of panic in the public, the security forces and the rescue services. The outrage was an announcement to the world that the IRA was still capable of mounting an offensive in the province, despite press utterances that they were 'becoming toothless'.

If we look at the obverse of the coin, the need for silence, then firearms are especially important. In some countries 'silencers' are illegal, in many countries they are not. Despite the legality or otherwise, it is not necessary to have a licence to acquire one. The word 'silencer' is a misnomer; true, it would be possible to almost completely silence a firearm but the result would be so unwieldy that its usage would be severely limited.

The silencer/suppressor is by no means new; they were available even before World War I from the American company owned by Hiram Maxim as well as from the UK (Parker-Hale and Hopkins & Allen). It was World War II with its plethora of special forces both official and unofficial with an increasing requirement to kill men, silently and at close ranges, which inspired the researchers to set out on the trail to produce more and more effective devices.

The absence of a driving post-war need did not halt private development. Sterling Arms of the UK eventually produced their silenced version of the tried and trusted SMG, which many authorities claim still stands as the ultimate suppressed sub-machine-gun. Heckler & Koch's MP5SD is a technical delight to operate. Yet it is in private workshops where devices of interest to the terrorist are more likely to be found. If this statement seems to imply a series of 'garden shed' engineers turning out suppressors for Qaddafi, nothing could be further from the truth.

It is a fact that such interested enthusiasts have proved that a reasonably effective sound suppressor for muzzle fitment can be turned out by any half-way decent engineer. Indeed poachers in Europe and the USA have for many years been using home-made devices to fit to small calibre (.22) weapons. A plastic container of the type used for washing-up liquid, stuffed with commercial steel wool of the pan-scouring variety, fixed with masking tape to the muzzle of a small-bore rifle, makes a very good sound and flash inhibitor. It is extremely limited in the number of shots which can be fired through it, but one is sorely pressed to find a cheaper device.

We have now reached the stage when suppressors of varying effectivenesses can be purchased as add-ons or supplementary conversion kits for a very wide range of weapons, all of which are favoured by the terrorist. A silenced or suppressed ability is of more concern to the assassin than to any other terrorist. The accurate, unheard shot has always been the nightmare of bodyguards. Unable to locate the source of gunfire by sight or sound, they are left in a vulnerable defensive posture, powerless to take offensive action. This gives the assassin, if he has chosen his vantage point with care, the ability for a two- or three-shot operation and it dramatically increases his chances of making good his escape.

Stand off capability.   The term stand off is military in origin and is used because it so clearly describes this factor. In this context we are mostly concerned with the use of explosives; these give the attacker, by a variety of means, the ability to control his act of devastation from a distance. A bomber can stand off and view the results in real time, read about it in the newspapers or watch it on television whilst enjoying his evening martini.

There are basically two types of explosive: high explosive which has a 'cutting' effect; and low explosives which 'push'. The latter are more common in mining and quarrying operations and, as such, in some parts of the world can be more easily obtained. High explosives, the modern 'plastiques', have specialised uses, many of them military. They can be precisely controlled, are stable to store and carry and give a tremendous size:effect ratio in value for money. There are a range of common ingredients to most explosives which make them vulnerable to detection by vapour analysing devices but these can, and often are, defeated. It is normally accepted that dogs will detect more reliably than the machines. Even better than the dog is the pig, but the pig is less easy to train in its personal habits; is no respector of religion or costs; and is generally less than welcome in a VIP airport lounge.

In terrorist operations there is a variety of home-made explosive mixtures; perhaps the best known are the 'co-op' and ANFO mixtures. Fertilisers (which are used for the nitrogen content) and diesel oil as a gelling agent have long been used by the IRA in areas where they are able to cram large amounts of the mix into culverts, milk churns and the like. The results are devastating.

Explosives are normally selected for their horrific effect and the fact that they offer a wide number of methods of remote detonation. Not all terrorists are martyrs by any means and high on the list of operational planning factors is the safe escape route.

One of the most spectacular bombings in recent years must have been the assassination of Admiral Luis Carrero Blanco, then the Prime Minister of Spain, and heavily tipped to follow in Franco's footsteps. A few days before 20 December 1973, a group of labourers had been diligently working away on a Madrid street, carrying out last minute repairs on a section of road which was to be used by the ministerial cavalcade. Unsuspected, the Basque militants, for that was their true identity, succeeded in making what was in effect an enormous culvert bomb. It was detonated with remarkable accuracy and actually hurled the Prime Minister's limousine clear over the top of the adjacent church. It was, claimed Basque militants, an act of revenge for the killing of a number of their comrades-in-arms.

In order to fire an electric detonator, all that is required is enough electrical power to heat a thin wire 'bridge' a fraction of an inch long for a period of time measured in milli-seconds; that shows just how small that source of power can be. Batteries for calculators and the like are easily available and quite sufficient for the job. Camera technology advances have resulted in so-called 'paper' cells only the thickness of a postcard but with the provision of ample power to fire a mini-detonator and thus initiate an explosive device.

The advent of quartz-controlled time-pieces has taken the bombers' art a quantum leap forward from the days of mainspring-driven watches, washing-machine timers and the like. It is now quite possible to plant an accurately timed bomb months ahead of the desired explosion time and to have the detonation accurate within seconds.

Perhaps one of the best known of such long-delay devices was placed in the Grand Hotel, Brighton. This was the town where the UK Conservative Party in power was to hold its Annual Conference. The Grand Hotel was chosen by many delegates, including the Prime Minister, Margaret Thatcher, as the place to stay. The bomb exploded on 12 October 1984 and, but for chance, could well have succeeded where Guy Fawkes failed and taken out the majority of the British Cabinet. As it was, five people were killed and many more injured seriously. If it did one salutory thing, it displayed the planning ability and the technical expertise of some members of the IRA. It is acknowledged in British police circles that the IRA numbers within its ranks some of the finest 'technicians' in the world.

It is not only timing devices which have been used to initiate horrific bombings. On 27 August 1979, in Warren Point, Northern Ireland, eighteen members of the 2nd Battalion, The Parachute Regiment ('the Red Devils'), were killed in a command-detonated explosive ambush. It was a technically brilliant operation and coincided with an explosion aboard the yacht of Earl Mountbatten of Burma, an uncle of the Queen. The bomb killed him as well as a number of others on board and created a backlash of public opinion rarely witnessed in the UK.

Even more frightening, and always disgusting because of the totally indiscriminate deaths, is the bomb which explodes on board aircraft. Various bomb data centres have stated that, potentially, one of the greatest exponents of the art is Abu Ibrahim, a nom-de-guerre, who has developed a very high degree of expertise in the use of barometric devices to control the initiation of suitcase bombs in the holds of aircraft.

Suitcase bombs are of course common and the evolution of adhesive sheet explosives, primarily designed for specialist military purposes, have revolutionised the 'art'. Detonators are now made in such miniature formats that on the cheaper brands of studded suitcase there is invariably enough natural metal with which to shield this component from the prying eyes of the security guards. Precautions against such attacks are obvious but at the same time commercially difficult. Stringent and thorough searching would bring major airports to a standstill and the person who would complain the longest would be the man at risk: the executive traveller.

At a personal and more precise level, no discussion on terrorist weapons could exclude the 'KGB assassin gun'. The poison gun of a score of sensational spy movies has been a reality for many years in the hands of KGB agents. Originally developed using cyanide pellets, there are a number of versions. From time to time a hit is made which catches the headlines. The most recent (publicised) case which certainly carries all the trademarks of a KGB removal operation was the killing of Georgi Markov in September 1979. Ricin poison was injected via the tip of an umbrella into his leg as he was travelling to work in London. He was a Bulgarian exile who worked for the Overseas Service of the BBC; motive enough for his elimination.

In conclusion, there are weapons favoured by terrorist groups, but they are unlimited in their full scope. The terrorist is often an ingenious animal, he is often courageous (just as often cowardly) and he invariably has a cause in which he fervently believes. Put these three ingredients together and you have a man who will use as a weapon anything he can get his hands on. Necessity – the mother of invention – was never set against a more pertinent backdrop.

10 The Technology of Terrorism

Terrorists' methods have advanced apace with every applicable and publicised technological breakthrough. The only defence against their continued advance is to deny them access to technical information. In itself this denial is an impossibility; inventors have to make money from their inventions and so do retail outlets. We live in a free society in which the public and potential purchaser is made aware of these advances through the advertising industry, trade journals and exhibitions. The terrorist in his many guises has access to all these information centres, if not directly, then by devious but easy routes. He is a versatile person often forced into lateral thinking in order to complete his task of terror and it is not necessarily into the arsenal of the arms manufacturer that he will delve for assistance. Many everyday domestic appliances offer him a means to an end in activating or disguising his deadly devices. In many cases he will be directly benefiting from Soviet technology which in pertinent areas is as advanced as that in the West. The terrorist has to be treated as if he has at least an equal knowledge to that of those security forces who oppose him. Latest advances in hard weapons technology is not all that important to the terrorist who is able to be just as lethal with unsophisticated and quite simple weapons. An exception to this may be the flow of weapons from Soviet hands into countries such as Libya which will eventually find their way into the terrorist arsenal. A similar situation could be said to exist with the sales of the more esoteric systems such as Exocet to Syria and both sides of the Iraq/Iran conflict. All three countries have terrorist organisations which they fund or sponsor.

On most occasions, though, the terrorist is confined to the use of weapons which can be fired without the need for launch gear of any kind. In this book we are considering only those targets where the travelling executive or diplomat can be said to be at risk. By definition, this precludes the large strategic and tactical targets which may one day soon become attractive to the terrorist and will make a significant difference to factors he considers when on the weapon acquisition trail. Within the context of this book, the advances in small arms ammunition, personal armour and methods of initiating explosives are the most pertinent topics. These are all important to the small group of fanatics bent on the targets which may affect the personal security of our readers. Great care has been taken in discussing these areas of development lest passive assistance should be given to the terrorist and it is for these reasons that no source is given or precise technical details described.

Nowadays when a terrorist organisation plans to hijack an aircraft or to conduct an operation which will eventually lead to their being secured in a 'stronghold' of some type with hostages at gun point, there is a fair chance that they will be anticipating an assault by security forces at some stage or another. Publicity, training by sophisticated instructors and common sense will have given them a good indication of the types of tactics and equipment likely to be used by the assault group. This will focus their minds at the planning and equipping stages of the operation into doing the best they can to nullify or avoid this assault threat. Not unnaturally the avenues open to them lie in killing the assault group, or making the situation so difficult that they cannot be assaulted without the certain death of the hostages. The latter, though, is unlikely to have much of an effect in some countries.

Scant importance was placed upon the lives of the hostages in Bogota, Colombia, when on 6 November 1985 security forces mounted an assault spearheaded by a tank on the Palace of Justice which was in the hands of M-19 terrorists. True, all the terrorists were killed, but so were over a hundred others including the President of the Supreme Court.

The education of the terrorist will include the effects of such devices as the now famous SAS 'stun grenade' and the various forms of tear gases. Neither of these options really present a problem to the terrorist if he anticipates their use; dark glasses and ear defenders severely dilute the effects of the former and temporary respirators are quite effective against the latter. Indeed there have been occasions where the effects of tear gas have been absolutely nil against the enemy who was benefiting from a full flow of adrenalin.

To alert the terrorist there is always an instant of warning prior to an attack and sadly this aspect has received a lot of publicity in a variety of books and articles resulting from the 1980 Iranian Embassy siege. The public (and therefore the terrorist) was told of the significance of 'bulges' in the walls and noises which indicated the attempts to infiltrate listening devices and pinhold lenses to conduct surveillance. He was shown the value of keeping television sets and the like switched on. If he has even this instant of warning, then he naturally looks to his arsenal to see what can be used to deter or delay the assault.

In terms of ammunition there is now a vast array of choice with which to blast through even the stoutest door and kill anybody standing behind. There is armour-piercing, teflon-coated, titanium-jacketed and explosive-tipped ammunition, and all are available on the open market. In the worst case, the terrorist knows that he may be faced with an attack by fully armed, well-equipped security forces, but he also knows that he can procure ammunition which will defeat the majority of body armour. Soft point and hollow point ammunition will stop the most determined soldier or policeman. All this is advertised and available.

Having said that there is ammunition which will defeat any body armour; the terrorist knows that in many countries strict adherence is still paid to the Geneva Convention and that those countries will not use ammunition which falls outside this convention. In the past this has tempted the terrorist to look to body armour and there is a remarkable variety of good workmanlike designs around which are both lightweight and unobtrusive offering him a reasonable level of protection. It is an area where great technical advances are continually taking place within the reputable companies. The last ten years has seen them go from steel to ceramics to kevlar to composites and back to ceramics as research progresses. Fortunately, most of the serious manufacturers apply rules almost as rigid as those applied to weapons in their sales of the most up-to-date garments.

When it comes to the subject of explosives, probably the most useful advance to the terrorist has been the development of the various forms of sheet explosive and linear cutting devices. The latter, which are based on the Monroe Effect,[1] are designed to allow very precise cutting of a variety of materials, developed to a fine degree to assist in space technology (the cutting away of redundant rocket motors and ejection seats); these charges are found more often in the suitcase of the saboteur than of the terrorist. The sheet explosives have, however, been put to good effect by the suitcase bomber. Due to the nature of the construction of the suitcase bomb it is rare for such objects to get through the efficient scrutiny of the experienced searcher who is supported by explosive vapour sniffers or, better still, dogs. In relatively unsophisticated airports, however and there are still too many of these, there is a fair chance that the bomb will pass inspection.

The true delight to the terrorist technician is the number of devices on the open market today which will allow him to ply his trade with great versatility when it comes to bomb construction. He has a truly remarkable choice when shopping for ingredients with which to arm his bombs and render them highly dangerous to the disposal specialist. More often than not the creation of a terrorist bomb is a team effort. The design specialist is too important to be risked at every stage of the process.

It is during the acquisition and manufacturing stage that the team is at its most vulnerable. The collection of the component parts may well be an operation carried out by a number of people who will not necessarily know the purpose of the items they have been instructed to buy. There is explosive to obtain, an initiation system of which the detonator is an essential part, timing devices, batteries, a container and construction materials. The role of the designer may end at the production of a very detailed drawing of the device and from there it could well pass into the hands of a man who packs the explosive into its camouflaged container which could be virtually anything. The firing circuit may be constructed by yet another party and inserted into the bomb container to make it ready all but for the final arming device, which could be anything from a simple safety pin to a sophisticated timing machine.

This final action system may control the arming of a number of 'anti lift' or 'anti tamper' devices: cells which will react to X-ray; cells which will react to light or the lack of light; the scope is only limited by the knowledge and experience of the designer. The main point is that there will usually be a safety 'switch' of some type to allow the bomb to be confidently carried by the man who is to place it – this will certainly not be one of the key men in the chain such as the designer or electrician. Because so many people are invariably involved, it creates a security weakness and the activity beforehand has often led to the capture of a cell due to the alertness of storekeepers or neighbours. Education in recognising these tactics is an important counter-measure in the overall battle against terrorism.

It would be wrong in the extreme to list all the everyday objects which are potentially of use to the bomber but suffice it to say that anything which provides power in an unobtrusive or miniaturised fashion; anything which offers accurate timing; anything which either makes or breaks a circuit as the result of a calculable action;

anything which changes size or shape to a predictable pattern under set conditions, all these systems and many, many more may be used by the skilled terrorist technician.

Security services and devices catalogues are a good source of information to the terrorist in more ways than one. Not only can he find the materials which he may want to use himself but he can also provide himself with a fairly accurate knowledge of what the security forces are likely to have. Those catalogues which also show the methods of use for their products will additionally be inadvertently giving the terrorist an idea of what to look for when he is locked in his stronghold with the hostages. If he knows what to look for and how to recognise the threat, he is quite capable of turning the tables on the intelligence agencies.

Possibly one of the most frightening aspects of the technology is the apparent ease with which a crude fission bomb could be constructed. Sources of information as easily infiltrated as a good public reference library will enable the part-skilled operator who has a reasonable physics background to construct such a device from the materials purchased at a hardware shop or supermarket. Considered opinion is that a person in the possession of a few kilograms of plutonium oxide (not as difficult to achieve as may be imagined) and a reasonable amount of good stable high explosive could build a device which would have a positive chance of exploding with the power of many tons of high explosive. Perhaps even more sobering is the thought that if a terrorist group can achieve this, it can also (and probably much more easily) construct biological and biochemical weapons.

It is of course highly unlikely that such weapons would be used by terrorists; certainly they would draw no support for their various causes were this to be the case. Generally the terrorist is not solely intent on killing people for the sake of it; their causes, in their eyes at least, have a chance of being recognised one day and the use of a nuclear device or a biochemical one to kill in the 'grand manner' would undoubtedly create such uncontrollable revulsion and disgust that it would not further the effort towards attainment of the goal.

What has to be considered is the possibility of the statement by a terrorist group that it is in possession of such a device. If the spokesman were to give a convincing and detailed explanation as to how they had constructed the bomb and where they had obtained the materials *and this explanation checked out*, where would the negotiator be? How do the police in less sophisticated countries actually decide whether they are dealing with a real situation or a masterly bluff?

There is no real need of course for the terrorist to resort to esoteric weapons if his requirement is to merely disrupt the forces of law and order. Any highly industrialised nation is extremely vulnerable, especially if industrial competitiveness is high on its list of priorities. The havoc created by attacks on gas pipelines, offshore oil rigs and governmental and commercial computer storage facilities can cause enormous economic problems in a surprisingly short space of time.

Use some of the sophisticated timing and explosive technology mentioned already and apply this to a situation which arose (not from a terrorist operation) in New York in 1977. There was an electrical blackout which lasted for two days. During that time an enormous amount of damage was done due to the loss of electrical power but what was particularly interesting was the near collapse of law and order. Arson and looting were carried out on a huge scale and it is difficult to see how the police could have coped if it had continued. Suppose that it had. Would the armed forces have been deployed? Almost certainly. New York is quoted just because it happened to occur there; it could be *made* to happen simultaneously in a score of cities with an even more dramatic effect and the perpetrator could be on a different continent by the time 'the bomb went off'.

In the fullness of time the terrorists will turn their attention to strategic targets. The effects of a hijack and bombing are still dramatic and always will be, but it is a fact that they remain in the media for shorter and shorter periods each time they occur. If this does prove to be the case then technological advances in missiles both ground-to-ground and ground-to-air will be of increasing interest to the terrorist.

It would not be a new technique. Certain cases have hit the headlines in the past. In 1973 the case of five Palestinians in Rome who were trying to bring down the El Al passenger aircraft with Soviet SA-7s was given a huge amount of publicity. A similar attempt took place in Paris in 1975 when a Yugoslavian aircraft was damaged. Sophisticated though these weapons may be, they seem to find their way into terrorist hands with monotonous regularity. It can only be a matter of time before the target strategy is re-addressed.

It is a fact that the Baader-Meinhof group threatened in the past to use a mustard gas on the civilian populace in an extortion attempt and it is equally well known that as early as 1975 a group of men were arrested in Austria during an operation in which they were in the process of synthesising nerve agents with the intention of selling these to an un-named terrorist group. So the seeds of the ideas are there and as technology progresses the means to deliver will become easier.

NOTE

1. The Monroe Effect relates to the calculation, lining and shaping techniques of explosive charges in a manner which produces a very precise cut. It relies on the chemical reaction from the explosion producing a molten 'slug' of metal from the lining material which penetrates the target substance; this penetration is followed up by superheated gases under great pressure which then forces the edges of the cut apart.

11 The Terrorist Fringe

'Meat is Murder'

Terrorism as we have seen is a methodology, it is a tool and a means, but it is not an ideology. It is a means which has increasingly been resorted to over recent years by a whole new 'subspecies' of direct action groups. The consumer orientated societies of the Western world have increasingly been plagued by extortion threats involving product contamination and other forms of direct actions which are criminal. These methods are used by what has come to be called the 'soft terrorists', but as we shall see there is nothing soft about the tactics of those who have radicalised environmentalism, animal rights and a host of other causes and crusades.

Such organisations, which we have preferred to call the 'terrorist fringe', are of course worthy of a book to themselves, so numerous are they and so potentially dangerous and destructive in the threat they pose. Had we written this book five years ago when such organisations were embryonic and peaceful in their intent, they would have hardly merited a mention. However, violence, once adopted, has its own momentum; legitimate protest has given way to direct action and criminal intent. Their inclusion is important to the completion of our study of the threat of the terrorist spectrum and this account will concentrate on two organisations in particular, one in Britain and the other in the United States, by way of illustration.

The British have always been known to be a nation of animal lovers. The amount spent on pet food alone would be more than enough to feed, clothe and pay the armed forces, or if you prefer would go a long way to resolving the short fall in the availability of renal dialysis machines. When the PIRA exploded a car bomb in the path of a ceremonial troop of Household Cavalry en route to mount guard at Horse Guards, the outcry equalled the protest which followed in the wake of the Harrod's bomb. National sympathy was directed not so much at the troopers, but at their horses.

It is hardly surprising, therefore, that animal rights movements have gained such notoriety in recent years. There are equivalents in Western Europe and the United States, whose citizens are just as dotty on their pets, but the movement in Britain is particularly virulent and nasty. Note the term which is used, the movement is about *rights* of animals and not their welfare. In Britain the Animal Liberation Movement is ten years old. Though terrorist in methodology it is not proscribed or illegal. Its declared enemy is anyone who uses animals, either for food or research. Since 98 per cent of the British population eat meat as a regular part of their diet, the movement does not lack targets. Butchers and battery farms, chemists which sell shampoos which have been tested on animals, shops selling fur coats and research laboratories are now in the front line of assault. Activists have hit slaughter houses, small research companies and the Royal College of Surgeons.

These establishments are attacked because the Animal Liberation Front believes that animals have an equal and parallel set of rights to human beings, in particular the same right to life as man. Nobody would deny that animals have a right to life. The argument lies on how much further animal rights extend. That animals are the same as humans is a claim which some of us find morally offensive, the activists use it as a moral base for terrorism. To claim that the slaughter of cattle in a market is on the same moral plane as the slaughter of those held in concentration camp by the Nazis, is at the very least a gross distortion and an insult to mankind. Eating a good steak may not be the best kind of food healthwise, and perhaps too much red meat does cause raised blood pressure. To claim however that such an indulgence makes the diner an accessory to torture and murder has as much justification as the claim by the activists to observe a higher morality to break the law.

By their own admission the Animal Liberation Front and its offshoots such as the Animal Rights Militia and Hunt Saboteurs have failed to win support through the normal channels open in a democracy, namely public argument and debate. Nevertheless the movement has attracted support and this provides funds which give an annual income estimated at over half a million pounds. Their money is used to back a new kind of politics with a hard terrorist edge, and witnessed by such statements as: 'If it is necessary to smash and destroy every butcher's shop in the land, the ALF will do it.'[1]

The ALF has an estimated 1300 hard core members in the field dedicated to action. The strength of the movement lies in its organisation, with small and autonomous cells scattered throughout the country. Such decentralisation makes it extremely difficult to penetrate the movement. It would appear the majority of the membership is female, almost all are under thirty years of age, recruited from middle-class white-collar jobs and professions. They number bank clerks, teachers and accountants among their membership who in all other respects are the very pillar of respectability.

The violence of their actions has escalated with frustration at their own failures to win over popular support. It is a trend one can identify in the pattern in violence for direct action from these 'new issue' groups, whether it be animal liberation or nuclear disarmament. The steps along that path of direct action which culminate in acts of terrorism can be identified as in Figure 11.1.

1 Demonstrations – attract attention
2 Obstruction/Confrontation
   (ambushing convoys carrying
   nuclear missiles)
3 Damage (from broken shop
   windows, bombs, arson)
4 Product Contamination
5 Intimidation
6 Personal Attack
7 Terrorism

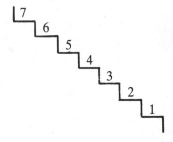

Figure 11.1   The escalating pattern of violence

In this pattern of violence, we tend to forget that their actions a few years ago appeared shocking enough at the time. In the northern border country the Hunt Retribution Squad desecrated a grave. In what was seen as a ghoulish act the grave of that English hunter of folk lore and song, John Peel, who had died a hundred and fifty years ago was disturbed and his remains scattered.

Elsewhere paint daubing and slogans gave way to attacks on property, acid attacks, and bricks through windows, and were accompanied by violent demonstrations. Now in the last five years a new pattern of violence has emerged which makes their earlier behaviour appear moderate by comparison. 'Every day our comrades and fellow animals stay behind bars their torment must be avenged even if this means some of the filth will lose their lives.'[2] Demonstrations failed, property attacks did not rally support, there are only people left. Letter bombs have been sent to party political leaders, the Prime Minister, the Cabinet and to the homes of leading scientists. In 1985 the ALF planted sixteen bombs as part of a nationwide campaign of destruction and intimidation in which two thousand acts of violence were committed and £6 million worth of damage caused.

One of their most spectacular was the Mars attacks. Two Mars chocolate bars in a Southampton store were contaminated with rat poison, and a warning telephoned to a national newspaper. In what was to prove a salutory lesson in crisis management techniques, the ill prepared company had no option other than to order the remains of three thousand tons of chocolate from the shelves. The loss in revenue was conservatively put at over three million pounds. Why did the ALF hit Mars? The Corporation funds dental research into tooth decay which uses monkeys.

The Hunt Retribution Squad struck. The grave of the recently deceased Duke of Beaufort, a Master of the Hounds, was desecrated. The ghouls threatened to send his head to Princess Anne.

'I hate them. I hate their red faces and their loud voices, sat up on their horses all superior expecting everyone to get out of the way. I'd like to see them killed.'[3] The speaker is a young advertising executive who has a pleasant home in Surrey and commutes everyday to smart offices in Mayfair, London. He is a prosperous member of the middle class; he is not poor, unskilled or unemployed, with grounds for a chip on his shoulder. He is what is now termed a 'Yuppie', and he means precisely what he says.

The living are now the targets, for the animal liberationists have turned against their own species. In a war which is now fought with a new intensity, there is a consistent theme of hate. One cannot escape the conclusion that it is less a love of animals and more a dislike of other human beings which is the motive force.

There are other and more disturbing trends in the Animal Liberation Front. Its founder is a man called Ronnie Lee, a committed anarchist. It is almost as if this one aspect of terrorism has turned full circle to that time in the nineteenth century when it was anarchist inspired. There is every reason to conclude that the movement has been infiltrated and radicalised by extremists from both the Left and the Right of the political spectrum.

Animal rights defies the rule books, and it is not unusual to see the black flags of the Anarchists alongside banners of the National Front at animal liberation demonstrations and protest marches, in which the wilder elements choose public confrontation. Anarchists are committed to causing violence and confusion in society at large and theirs is the politics of revolution: 'Animal Liberation must be part of a wide spectrum of revolutionary change, for British democracy is based on more blood and terror than any other country.'[4]

The Animal Rights Militia storm designated targets in daylight. Several hundred hooded raiders will attack a laboratory, occupy the premises and commit as much damage as they can. Some have been caught, a few are now in prison, but this appears to be no real deterrent. Indeed laboratories and other potential targets have become 'high tech' fortresses, capable of withstanding even the most determined assaults. The most chilling example of the current campaign was a bomb placed under a scientist's car. That it did not explode was an accident, or divine providence, depending on your viewpoint. The ALF gave no warning. They had intended to kill. Violence against researchers who experiment using animals is likely to increase, and this is a trend which one can identify throughout the Western world. Scientists are being intimidated by a carefully orchestrated barrage of hate designed to terrorise their lives, at work and at home.

In September 1986 the subject of intimidation and terrorism appeared on the agenda of no less a prestigious body than the British Association for the Advancement of Science. This was discussed at great length during their annual conference held at Bristol University amidst unprecedented scenes of tight security. Some expressed their concern and fear, saying they were unwilling to publish the findings or details of their research lest this attracted the attention of the terrorists. Working in a climate of fear is hardly conducive to research and if they do not publish their results, the knowledge gained cannot be so readily shared with others for the mutual benefit of all.

It became apparent too that personal attacks were made not against those who conducted experiments, but rather those scientists who spoke out against the liberationists. Many scientists spoke of their concern for the welfare of the animals but in this of course they missed the point. The ALF is not interested in animal welfare, but in their rights, equal to that of human beings.

There is a similar disturbing pattern in escalation which can be detected in the peace movements and the environmentalists. These are both examples of genuine popular protest with as many as two million supporters in Western Europe who have been radicalised and exploited by others. Debate is healthy and dissent a cherished feature of democracies, provided it is expressed within the laws of the land. At the same time anything which attacks the solidarity of NATO and threatens the cohesion of the Atlantic Relationship has the blessing of Moscow. The peace movements may well be funded in some indirect fashion by the Kremlin, and it may be a coincidence that some leading members of these organisations are card-carrying members of their national communist parties. But the peace movement is one-sided. There are no reported episodes of the women of Kiev protesting about the nuclear weapons around their city.

The disturbing feature is not just the escalation in violence or the costs to the taxpayer of the extra precautions needed to counter direct actions; but the documented evidence is of attacks made on defence industries in conjunction with the Euroterrorist movements. Factories and military bases have been attacked and it is clear that the protest groups are being exploited, probably unwittingly, by Action Directe, RAF, CCC and other terrorist groups.

Nor are governments above reproach when it comes to incidence of terror. The French attack on a Greenpeace ship *Rainbow Warrior* in New Zealand was as blatant an act of terror, state-sponsored terror, as any underwritten by Libya.

In November 1986 two whalers were scuttled in Reykjavik harbour. Icelandic police described the scuttlings as deliberate acts of sabotage and responsibility was claimed by the radical Sea Shepherd animal rights group. This movement broke with Greenpeace some years ago. At about the same time a man using a public lavatory in an English provincial town was badly injured by a booby-trapped bomb. The toilets in question had gained notoriety because they were frequented by homosexuals. The catalogue of these and other bizarre incidents increases day by day.

In the United States fringe terrorism takes a number of forms. The Ku Klux Klan occasionally emerges in the Southern States with its sick racial hatreds. The key to Klan morale and unity, in the immediate aftermath of the Civil War and today, is the hatred some whites have for blacks. In those communities where it now rears its head it is because it has sufficient support, either because it is admired or feared.

Environmentalists have resorted to direct action and this will frequently take the form of a mass protest leading to confrontation with the authorities. On emotive issues like nuclear power there is that same disturbing escalation in violence, and radicalisation in aims and objectives. Product extortion (whereby companies are held to ransom against the threat of their product being contaminated) by both criminals and the protest movement have appeared as isolated incidents, although considerable harm and distress has been caused with people being killed.

The more obvious trends today are to be found in the hard core politics of the ultra right. Clinics which offer abortion have been subjected to arson attacks by those who claim allegiance to the 'Right to Life' and similar movements. Other organisations use theology to justify violence and racism. In this context the Christian Identity Movement has proved increasingly troublesome and militant in recent years. Blending their hatred of Blacks and Jews they both preach and practise armed violence to achieve their goals. It is an explosive combination of religion and racism spread by means of public access cable television to perhaps five thousand hard-core members and several times that in supporters. It is a movement which originated in the mid-West where its strength is still concentrated. The Federal Government in Washington comes in for its special share of hatred; dubbed ZOG (Zionist Occupationist Government) it is blamed for all America's ills. In recent years the movement has attracted new adherents in bankrupt farmers who have no love of federal government. Militants have bombed, robbed banks and raided National Guard Armouries. The organisation lacks cohesion and strong leadership, but is skilled in weapons and explosives. The Christian Identity Movement and its umbrella organisation The Aryan Nation are also linked to Posse Comitatus, another mid-Western group of violent tax-protest vigilantes.

None of these groups is strong enough to cause any real problems at the present time, but they were all extremely well armed and proficient in the use of weapons. Many embittered veterans of the Vietnam War have been attracted to their cause and this has helped not only to swell their numbers but to improve on skills.

In the Western world, protest movements have become radicalised and violent, committed to terrorist acts because in a system of permanent consensus over issues which they regard as important, such as killing and experimentation on animals, there can be no real chance for change by peaceful means.

NOTES

1. *Animal Liberation Front Bulletin*, no. 11, 1985.
2. *Animal Liberation Front Bulletin*, no. 11, 1985, quoted in 'Brass Tacks', BBC2 TV, 19 June 1986.
3. *Independent*, 14 November 1986.
4. *Animal Liberation Front Bulletin*, no. 11, 1985.

12 The Media and Terrorism

'The newspaper is of necessity something of a monopoly, and its first duty is to shun the temptations of monopoly. Its primary office is the gathering of news. At the peril of its soul it must see that the supply is not tainted. Neither in what it gives, nor in what it does not give, nor in the mode of presentation, must the unclouded face of truth suffer wrong. Comment is free but facts are sacred.'

Manchester Guardian, 6 May 1926

Violence is news, of that there is no dispute; that a free press is as critical to the continuation of a free and just democratic society as are the laws of the land and a freely elected government is equally indisputable. 'Comment is free but the facts are sacred'; the above quotation pre-dates television and was written only six years after the first commercial radio broadcast, yet the principle stands as true in 1987 as it did in 1926. What event was the precursor to the *Guardian* printing that comment is lost in the mists of time but it seems likely that similar arguments raged then as do today about the role of the media. The significant difference is that the sheer potency of the modern media has escalated the intensity of the debate by a quantum leap.

The responsibility of the media is plain: to present the facts. Analysis and opinion perhaps belong in the editorial columns and interview sessions, though this distinction is not quite the easy, clear-cut business it may appear. The television camera has been described as the 'eye of truth' and, in that it cannot lie and truly records events as they occur, it should be recognised as becoming the actual eye of the observer without necessarily possessing the peripheral perspective so important to a rounded picture. For instance, soldiers on the Northern Ireland scene in the days of the full-scale street riots will not forget the experience of re-living on screen the events after one of those sessions when the camera filmed from behind the rioters. Gone are the shots of petrol bombs and bricks being hurled towards the camera; all that is seen now is the menace of the helmeted, armoured soldiers advancing with batons and riot guns. The situation is the same but the presentation and possible interpretation is totally different yet it is still the truth; it is literally another point of view, another perspective. Yet who can blame the observer for harbouring a feeling that the army is being too aggressive and inflammatory? Who can blame the cameraman? He is recording reality not fantasy.

Reporters and cameramen are human and as such have political inclinations and personal feelings; it would be difficult to accept that they are totally free from bias. Generally, unless it is 'hot' news in real time from an incident, reports are given editorial scrutiny before they go on the air and the fairest possible picture is usually painted. Yet this examination, even if exercised to the ultimate degree of care, does not rob the media, and especially television, of its propensity for assisting the terrorist.

To have an assassination described in the newspaper, no matter how competent the journalist may be, requires concentration and imagination on the part of the reader in order to conjure up the reality of the situation. To have a hijack assault described on the radio is no more dramatic than listening to a cup final football match. Put the aftermath of a bomb incident on the television, show the riot in the Falls Road, Belfast, and record the terrorist making his demands from the stronghold in the Embassy and this is real; it is in the living room. There is no call for imagination – it is there beside your own hearth.

The television camera is capable of magnifying the potency of violence many times over by taking the terrorist to an audience vastly superior in numbers, and in a much more dramatic fashion, than he could ever have hoped for. It is a weapon in his hands on occasions, yet even then it is still performing the role that the public demands – bringing in the 'truth'. It is fair to use the term weapon for the media, an unwitting weapon perhaps, but many of the aspects of psychological warfare are based on media manipulation; a manipulation of which the organs of the media may be completely unaware. Take this a step forward and assume that as we are right and terrorism *per se* is wrong; why should we not use that weapon as we would any other in the armoury and turn it to our own defensive and offensive strategies?

If one of the desperate needs of any terrorist group is to achieve publicity so that their message and cause can be broadcast to the world (and it should be remembered that most terrorist groups firmly believe that they are right and that time and effort will achieve their desired final redress of grievance), would a governmental or self-imposed 'D-Notice' on all terrorist incidents have the effect of 'starving out' violence? Would it have the opposite effect of escalating violence to such a horrifying degree that there was simply no way that the media could *afford* to ignore it? Would this be the Catch-22 of modern times?

The television coverage of the Munich episode when the action finally took place at Furstenfeldbrück airfield, showed the disaster in all its stark detail. The public outcry in West Germany and the rest of Europe was severely embarrassing to a government which had actually done the right thing in essence, however the cameras recorded only the truth of the events. They were not privy to the soul-searching of the decision makers, the unease on the part of the police or the determination of the Israeli government.

The assault by the SAS on the Iranian Embassy has been described as television's 'golden hour' and so perhaps it was. The public saw an exciting and efficient assault taking place; they heard gunshots and explosions and about ten minutes later they saw hostages being bundled out of the doors unharmed. Days later they began to read in the newspapers of soldiers shooting terrorists who had already laid down their arms. This was possibly true and there would have been sound reasons for this taking place in the interests of the overall mission, which was to ensure the safety of the hostages. The man in the street nodded wisely and said 'Quite right. It had to be done'. But this would have had a markedly different reception if the television cameras had been inside the rooms and the public had seen it taking place. Sitting in armchairs and watching, without witnessing the tension of the build-up to the attack, without knowing the degree of training of the soldiers, in ignorance of the political insistence that no hostages should be risked, without knowledge of the 'hidden grenade' tactics of Middle East terrorists and without the benefit of the troops' briefings; there would have been sympathy for the downed terrorists and shouts of 'unfair play'. Yet once more what they would have seen would have been an accurate record of events.

The Balcombe Street siege in London in December 1975 is a prime example of how the weapon of the media can be turned to good effect during a terrorist incident. For five days the siege had been under way; four gunmen of the IRA had fled to the Balcombe Street apartment after shooting up a Mayfair restaurant. As hostages they had the elderly couple who owned the apartment. On Day 6 of the operation, the Metropolitan Police erected a high hessian cloth screen to block off the streets (and the cameras) from view and it was casually 'leaked' to the press that the SAS were on their way to move in on the gunmen. This went on the air; shortly afterwards the four gunmen surrendered. There had been no gunfire from the police throughout the whole incident. It was a classic resolution. The IRA men were jailed for life and this has to be a far better deterrent than four dead 'martyrs'.

Probably one of the most contentious issues in the media–terrorist debate of this century was the BBC's decision to release the interview with a member of the Irish National Liberation Army (INLA) in July 1979. Until they claimed responsibility for the murder of Airey Neave, Member of Parliament and Shadow Secretary of State on 30 March 1979, very few people had even heard of the INLA. David Lomax, a BBC interviewer, succeeded in penetrating the INLA and managed to get a recorded interview. The unnamed interviewee justified the killing with a rambling speech full of communist clichés, accusations that Neave was a torturer and a general criticism of British society. Neither the police nor the government was informed of the existence of the recording which, after a great deal of internal debate within the BBC, went on the air on 5 July. The response in the short term was surprisingly moderate. There were no protests, with the exception of Lady Neave, Airey's widow, who happened to be watching television at the time and not surprisingly was very distressed. The *Daily Telegraph* published a strong, critical letter from her. Shortly after, the subject became the focal point for searching and angry debate in the media itself and in political circles. The BBC's justification was that the public had a right to hear the views of the terrorists and that if these were covered up it could be an encouragement for the terrorists to 'speak' more and more with violence.

In this incident, the fact remains that what had been a relatively unheard-of group was suddenly presented with an audience of millions before which they were able to express their views. There is a school of thought that this interview could have inspired the bombing of Earl Mountbatten's boat on 27 September 1979 in which he and three others died; the theory being that this was a desperate attempt by the PIRA to match the amount of INLA publicity.

So, if the news media is to be viewed as a weapon it should probably be regarded as a rifle with no safety catch and a slightly bent barrel which can go off at any time and gives no accurate indication of where the shots are likely to land. This is not an over-simplification; in the examination of the newsworthiness of such an interview, the potential effects have to be examined from every conceivable angle lest the unexpected 'ricochet' occurs.

Probably the finest exponent of the art is the Soviet KGB. Disinformation is currently believed to be under 'Directorate A' of the KGB which carries the overall responsibility for Propaganda and Psychological Warfare. Disinformation is defined by the KGB as: 'The dissemination (in press, radio and television) of false information with the intention to deceive public opinion.' When the department was formed in 1967 by the then KGB Chairman General Yuri Andropov, it went into 'overdrive' and is currently reckoned to be handling somewhere in the region of 800–1000 active deception operations annually.

The greatest ploy used by the Directorate in its work (and arguably it is at least partly effective) is the evocation of guilt within the Free World. In particular the target is the USA. One has only to look at the number of communist-influenced groups who attacked the development of the neutron bomb. Lurid 'pictures' were conjured of Soviet cities, their buildings intact while the citizenry lay dead in their millions. The neutron bomb was in fact a design for a small pinpoint weapon to be used in defence behind Allied lines in Western Europe in the event of a Soviet 'over-run'. The Soviet propaganda machine also aims to make us feel guilty for being successful, wealthy, over-fed and enjoying a high standard of living whilst the poor terrorist born into poverty is only trying to achieve what the reader has already got due to his forefather's hard work! Most dealings in the world of KGB disinformation are via the obvious links of the press agency *Novosti*, the official news service TASS and Radio Moscow.

One of the roles of another supposed major contributor, the World Peace Council, is the influencing of public opinion in the democratic countries of the Free World. Methods are as old as the hills: a reliance to a degree on journalists who already have an 'inclination to the left' (and there are many), and the KGB wining and dining of Moscow correspondents where they are fed vodka, borscht and baloney in equal proportions, which will result in the more gullible reporters submitting the required articles.

There have certainly been concerted and consistent attacks on weapon development programmes in the USA and Europe by groups of journalists and organisations of the type such as Mobilisation for Survival, Coalition for New Foreign and Military Policy, the International League for Peace and Freedom and the Campaign for Nuclear Disarmament. Trident, the B-1, the Neutron bomb, 'Star Wars', the deployment of US nuclear weapons in Europe and many others have come under fire. A degree of success has to be imagined as some of the programmes would appear to have been stopped.

If so much money is spent on disinformation by the KGB to follow through the strategies outlined in brief above, then it is probable that some of that money is also diverted into the effort to support the terrorist in the media. It trains, or organises the training of, so many diversified groups of terrorists and guerrillas that it is unimaginable that the effort would fall short of this much easier and less attributable form of support.

There is surely a case in some particular instances of terrorist action for a committee decision to allow the press to be a party to deliberate and calculated misinformation in the very short term if hostage lives are to be saved. Such a tactic would not be without its dangers of course; would it destroy the public trust, such as it is, in the accuracy of the press and would it lead to a situation over a period of time where the 'Balcombe Street' option would not work?

It has frequently been stated by media professionals that the viewing public hungers for horror. There does seem to be a pathological need on occasions for the man at his fireside to feel that he is in the front line regardless of the incident being reported. There is a personal thrill and a 'What if I were there' feeling related to the reality of the event and not necessarily the causation of it. Nonetheless, the media has to fill this need in the public and regardless of the individual interpretations, it is fulfilling its function so long as the truth is being reported in an unbiased fashion.

13 The Terrorist Threat Today

Before we examine the various responses to terrorism, it would be as well to pause for a moment and look at the threat which is posed today. If we were to measure the threat by the amount of attention terrorism attracts from the media then the prognosis would indeed be a dismal one. The problem is that our present notions and impressions of terrorism are all formed and moulded not through the study of history, or the influence of tradition, but in a large measure by the media. This explains too why terrorists, in their war against the West, devote so much of their strategy and their efforts to capturing the attention of the media and using it for their own purposes.

To listen to the media is to believe that terrorism is 'the cancer' of the contemporary world and, despite appearances, this is manifestly not the case. Nevertheless, the media today, or at least large segments of it, is living proof of those terrorists who are very successful at generating enormous publicity for the minimum physical effort. Terrorism flourishes in the free and open societies of Western democracies, and poses a very real problem for many organisations and individuals. In the recent past some countries, notably Turkey and Italy, have been in danger from terrorists, but though society is very vulnerable, no democracy is threatened by terrorism.

A strange feature of the modern world is the resilience of states to survive pressures and setbacks; and this is particularly true of democracies. The power of the state, with the vast resources at its command, is always greater than that which can be deployed by the terrorist. In the case of both West Germany and Italy, the terrorist menace which had swept to such prominence through organisations like Baader-Meinhof and the Red Brigades, were later subdued to manageable proportions by national policies and concerted, co-ordinated efforts on the part of the various agencies.

Elite terrorist groups are unlikely to survive intact and conduct operations at will when confronted by the full panoply of state power when that is mobilised by a democracy roused to anger. Nationally inspired terrorist movements such as those in Spain and Northern Ireland are able through their appeal to a segment of the population to be more resilient, but even PIRA and ETA no longer appear to be the force they once were.

In theory the state ought to succeed, but in practice it frequently makes heavy weather of combating terrorism, and this is for a variety of reasons. The plethora of law enforcement agencies, counter-terrorist units and special forces, intelligence organisations and the inter-service rivalries between the police and the military, make the task of co-ordination and integration of effort much harder than it need be. At the same time governments can often bring additional terrorist problems upon themselves. As we have seen, terrorism is increasingly a product not of repression and totalitarianism, but of liberalism and democracies. It is a fact that since the death of Franco the incidence of both crime and terrorism in Spain has increased. If we follow this line of argument further it leads us to the rather unsavoury observation that in countries such as France and West Germany, Portugal and Turkey, the incidence of terrorism increased under administrations that are to the left of centre in the political spectrum.

Governments can and do defeat terrorism. There are a number of means open to them but one certainly is a response which is ruthlessly and totally efficient. After 1981 the Ayatollah Khomeini found that his regime was opposed by the Mujahedeen of the left who formed an alliance with some like-minded political parties. This opposition quickly erupted into a particularly nasty terrorist campaign which for a while at least was also remarkably successful. In the space of three months they managed to kill a prime minister, about half of the members of the ruling Council, sundry chiefs of police and members of parliament by the score. By that time it was the turn of the Ayatollah to turn nasty and to respond with unrestrained brutality. Police and security forces killed without discrimination, information was tortured out of suspects and within a further three months they had broken the back of the resistance. Other states have achieved an equal degree of success, with far less brutality, and over a longer period of time.

The problem on the international front is that governments and their agencies are trying to co-ordinate their policies and actions in response to a threat which does not have a consensus definition. A publication[1] lists 109 different definitions of terrorism in the last half-century. In our research we have come across one or two new definitions from the United States government, and even more from Western Europe, all different.

In so far as we are concerned, terrorists are people who in the name of what they consider to be lofty moral causes engage in indiscriminate acts of violence. Terrorism waged in democracies is the deliberate and systematic murder, maiming and menacing of the innocent to inspire fear for political ends. The terrorism we experience today began as a trend in the late sixties where it took hold as an extension of radical politics, or national and separatist movements. Now it has become an international phenomenon.

When it comes to dealing with international terrorism there is a wide discrepancy between the strong speeches and rhetoric of government leaders and spokesmen, and the inaction, or at best weak action that follows. Since the terrorist is out to destabilise democratic societies, and to show that their governments are impotent, the weak response does reinforce the case. There are some governments who will stand up to the terrorist threat and respond with vigour and purpose. The British view is particularly hardline and uncompromising. Governments should refuse to deal with terrorist organisations and their government backers, even at the price of civilian casualties. There is an Englishman supposedly on the list of hostages in the Lebanon; supposedly because although his name is included in the communiqués issued by Islamic Jihad, there is no other evidence to say he is alive.

Notwithstanding the personal anguish of the man and his family, London has implemented its policies. When faced with the evidence presented at a terrorist trial which was enough to convince a jury of Syrian duplicity and involvement, the Foreign Office responded quickly. The Syrian Ambassador and his embassy staff had blatantly breached diplomatic protocol and behaviour. Britain severed diplomatic relations with Syria, arguably the *de facto* Arab power in the Middle East, and looked to the European Community for concerted action. The best Britain can expect is a mild slap on the wrist. France as ever will play the pragmatic game as the one European state which is heavily committed to Middle Eastern affairs, by virtue of history and by the need to secure the freedom of its men held hostage.

As the scandal of Irangate unfolds, it is the United States which has proved the greatest shock, and for many the biggest disappointment. The brave promises of President Reagan and the warnings he issued to terrorists who attacked American citizens are now placed into their true context of plenipotentiaries despatched to Tehran bearing tribute to the Ayatollah. Iran is a country which has held American hostages for 444 days, constantly refers to the United States as the 'Great Satan', and is generally regarded as having fomented some of the worst terrorist outrages against American citizens and property overseas. Selling arms to Iran via Israel, Japan or wherever, has infuriated the Europeans, and angered moderate Arabs such as Saudi Arabia and the Gulf States who live in daily fear from Iranian sponsored Shi-ia fundamentalist violence. In this instance terrorism has achieved its objective. It sets out to terrorise, and to provoke its target into irrational promises. The actions by the US National Security Council can be considered as irrational in their attempt to win back those citizens held hostage in the Lebanon. The irony is that the principal negotiator for their release is an Englishman, Terry Waite, the envoy of the Archbishop of Canterbury. Waite, too, has become a hostage presumably of those with whom he negotiated in the past for, at the time of writing, little beyond rumour and speculation is known of his whereabouts.

Iran, Libya, Syria and other governments set the pace in one aspect of terrorism today which is potentially the most damaging of all; state-sponsored terrorism. This is a high-value, low-risk undertaking which for some governments has assumed the proportions of warfare by proxy. The state sponsors who orchestrate violence at a safe distance make their gains, not from the physical acts themselves, but from our reactions to them.

State-sponsored terrorism is mainly the instrument of dictators with ambitions and egos greater than can be satisfied by their national image and power base. The sponsors of international terrorism resemble in many respects children trying to find out by trial and error how far they can go in provoking the adults until punishment is meted out, or they are appeased into behaving differently. Some states like Syria will hide behind a sequence of front men and subterfuge, always ready to deny their guilt and protest their innocence. Others like Libya claim they have the right to sponsor acts of violence in the territory of another state. This in part explains why Europe is so popular as a terrorist battlefield. Israel is the real enemy for Middle Eastern terrorism, but it is difficult to penetrate. The United States, though Israel's closest ally, is a long way away and terrorist attacks there might well be too provocative and in any case there are plenty of Americans in Europe. Up until a few years ago the most popular American target was the defence installations. That has begun to change as they have become increasingly well fortified and so the terrorist, both international and indigenous, has turned his attention to the commercial sector.

So where does this leave the international traveller? The state is concerned and the need to respond to the terrorist with effective resources at the international level has become apparent; but at the same time governmental actions will not, and probably cannot, guarantee to protect the individual and his property. Government response has improved considerably but terrorist incidents have been increasing at a rate of between 12 per cent and 13 per cent annually over the past ten years. In 1984 there were 21 terrorist attacks on American businesses and executives overseas. The people who were caught up in these attacks had good cause to be terrified. There were 28 killed and 74 wounded. The damage to property amounted to $22 million. In 1985 36 attacks were carried out on American business interests overseas. In Europe the favoured weapon is the bomb. The terrorist uses bombs because they are easy to build, easy to conceal and they do not require the terrorist to be around when they detonate.

American banks and computer companies have been popular targets for terrorists dedicated to fighting what they view as Yankee economic imperialism. In Belgium, West Germany and the United Kingdom it is companies in the defence field, and especially those involved in such highly contentious programmes as Cruise missiles, which are selected for attack.

For travellers in the Middle East, the abiding fear at present is the aircraft hijack, especially when flying on some of the local national airlines. The immediate answer in this instance is to choose the airlines of those countries which have no political role to play in the conflicts of the region. Swiss Air, KLM, SAS and some of the Far Eastern carriers all maintain an extensive transregional network.

In Latin America, followed closely by Europe and the Middle East, the major threat comes from kidnapping. From the early 1970s through to the present day 190 different groups have conducted hostage seizures. In that period ransom demands have been levelled against 56 countries and 46 business corporations. Those most often victimised are, in descending order, citizens from the United States, France, Great Britain, West Germany and Italy; these countries alone account for approximately half of all known hostage cases.

Corporations react in different ways. Some will agree a financial figure and calculate that once protective measures against terrorist attack exceed, for example, 1 per cent of their turnover, it is time to call it a day and withdraw from that particular country. Even so, executives have to live under very trying and restrictive circumstances as illustrated by one American businessman living in Bogota: 'The stuff I have to go through to protect myself and the family is worse than the terrorists. The last people my wife and I see at night are my goons, and they're the first I see in the morning.'[2]

The situation is unlikely to get better, and in our view it will get worse. Terrorism is not new in history, and even this century has witnessed more than its fair share; but today's terrorism differs in its extent and its violence. The terrorists' strategy is premised on the ability to hit even harder in the future, no matter what precautions the state may take to protect its people and their property. The fear and intimidation that terrorism thrives on in its parasitic existence are totally dependent upon this threat.

In order to counter such fear the international traveller needs the knowledge and understanding of the terrorist threat so that he may minimise the risk to himself and to his family; and should he find himself caught up in an incident, whether by accident or design, know how to survive.

NOTES

1. Alex Schmid, *Political Terrorism: A Revised Guide* (New Brunswick, NJ: Prentice-Hall, 1984).
2. As quoted in *Fortune*, January 1986.

Part III

The Government Response to Terrorism

14 International Law and Terrorism

The citizen can look to the law of his land for protection. Laws will not of their own accord eradicate crime, but they do offer the individual redress and comfort. Beyond the state and its boundaries, however, there is little comfort for the international businessman and frequent traveller; and this is because international laws are not the same as those enacted by a state.

The state is sovereign. It has, in theory at least, the absolute power to pass and enforce the law in accordance with its constitution. All terrorism is criminal in the eyes of the government which is attacked, to be punished with the full force of the law or the miscreants hurriedly extradited into another's domain before they can cause any more trouble. National laws, especially those against terrorism, don't necessarily prevent terrorism, but at least they do give the citizen some protection and the right of redress.

International law is different. It invariably takes the form of treaties or conventions signed by states, but it cannot have the force of national law, because states cannot accept any authority greater than their own. This is the meaning of sovereignty and it is something which states guard jealously and uphold rigorously. Neither is there any means by which a law, internationally passed and recognised by all, can be enforced, short of sanctions or warfare. There is no international police force, and the International Court of Justice at the Hague is as much cynically used and abused by the world as it is respected and honoured.

The law is in a sad condition when it comes to dealing with terrorists and international terrorism. Even the state record is pretty abysmal. Terrorists are killed and some are captured. Few of the latter are ever brought to trial but instead they are quietly despatched abroad to a safe haven. Georges Ibrahim Abdallah, self-confessed leader of one of Lebanon's most vicious terrorist gangs, and implicated in a number of assassinations in Europe, was tried and sentenced to four years by the French High Court. Here was a prime example not of the punishment fitting the crime, but of justice being subordinated to the greater public interest. It was clearly the French government's intention originally to rid themselves of

Abdallah as quickly as possible, but the due process of law intervened. The result was a horrific bombing campaign by terrorists in the autumn which left the city reeling with shock but at the same time determined not to succumb to such pressures. Abdullah has subsequently been tried and sentenced to life imprisonment for his crimes. There are other instances where terrorists serving prison sentences are exchanged for hostages in a subsequent terrorist episode. Few terrorists, except in such hardline countries as Britain, Israel and the United States, are likely to serve the full term of punishment.

It is not that the international community has not tried to get its act together. Terrorism has been with us for a very long time, and there has been the occasional flurry of diplomatic activity in an effort to contain and control the violence. A number of conventions have been battled through the General Assembly of the United Nations and even signed by the members; but none have been ratified by all and thus have no hold, not even moral persuasion, over the signatories. All of this simply goes to show the influence that terrorist organisations and their state sponsors have over such prestigious forums as the United Nations should not be overestimated.

In 1972 the massacres at Munich and Lod airports propelled the United Nations into action. That autumn, Secretary-General Kurt Waldheim exercised his special powers to initiate a debate in the General Assembly on 'Measures to prevent terrorism and other forms of violence which endanger or take innocent human lives or jeopardise fundamental freedoms.' It has to be said that very little progress has been made since that date. It did not help matters that Israel was the target of the two terrorist incidents that sparked off the world concern; but the malaise was deeper. In the United Nations attitudes towards terrorism fragment in the main along the traditional North/South divide. Most of the developing nations maintain the legitimacy of armed struggle 'against colonialist regimes and other forms of alien domination'.

The Soviet Union and its Eastern Bloc satellites espouse such causes too, but for different reasons. The developing nations cherish their belief in the inalienable right to self determination, but so do most right-thinking Western states though we tend to draw the line when it comes to violence. Others not only accept terrorism but would deem it a lawful act in the pursuit of liberation. It is this strident lobby in the United Nations which has sought exemption for acts of violence committed in the cause of national liberation. This means that any terrorist group which is able to command a measure of sponsorship or support in the General Assembly can buy immunity from legislation.

The result is that international law exerts an influence on terrorism in two directions, and, in so far as the frequent traveller is concerned, neither of them good. The first is a negative influence, since actions against terrorists are precluded. The second is even more deadly, for international law can on occasion discriminate positively – in favour of terrorists! Much of the problem and difficulties centre around the thorny question of extradition; an issue which we have already seen to create friction between states which are otherwise friends.

Extradition treaties between states, for traditional reasons contain exclusion clauses for those offences which are identified as 'political conduct'. Northern Ireland is a province which has been in political turmoil for close on twenty years in the current crisis. During that time the insurgents have drawn comfort and support, and its men on the run found public sanctuary, in the United States. When the United Kingdom has applied for extradition, American lawyers have been able to argue that since an 'uprising' existed in Northern Ireland, all crimes committed as part of the revolt were 'political' and thus the fugitives were exempt. No one would question the need for a democracy to provide sanctuary to the victims of oppression; and to many the members of the American Bar Association are indeed serving the highest tenets of their profession.

To those of us on this side of the Atlantic, however, it would appear that our allies have conveniently forgotten that Northern Ireland is part of a democracy where the opportunity for change by peaceful means is available. The more cynical would also note that American judges, political appointments all, have the need to be mindful of the votes won or lost through the vociferous celtic fringe. In 1986 President Reagan slipped into the fray and signed a Supplementary Treaty of Extradition which allowed the United States to narrow the political exemption clauses to exclude most acts of violent crime. He then used his considerable charm and powers of persuasion to ensure that the Senate would not subvert his initiative.

Sometimes extradition of a notorious terrorist is just too hot to handle for some states. Abu Abbas, high on Washington's wanted list of international terrorists was allowed to leave by the Italians in the messy days that followed the interception of an Egyptian airliner, despite the American attempt to have him extradited.

The *Achille Lauro* affair has invoked considerable speculation as to whether the terrorists are pirates. The laws against piracy have a long and respectable tradition of interstate co-operation across the centuries. Many eminent international jurists are under no doubt that seizing the *Achille Lauro* was piracy under the law of nations. The cruise liner was Italian registered and crewed, which means the terrorists are felons under Italian law. Mr Klinghoffer, an American citizen, was brutally killed, and other American passengers were robbed, which makes the miscreants felons under United States laws. The trial of the captured terrorists was held in Genoa. In July 1986 the court handed down its verdict. All were found guilty but eleven received substantially less than the maximum sentence allowed. These terrorists were treated with leniency because of their 'youth' and because they had grown up in the 'tragic conditions that the Palestinian people endure'. In the precise terminology of Italian law, the two judges and six-man jury held that the *Achille Lauro*'s seizure was indeed an act of terrorism; but the assailants were not classified as an 'armed band'. This meant that the hijackers were tried and sentenced as guerrillas or freedom fighters rather than criminals.

In so far as the United Nations is concerned the issue is not in doubt. Piracy is defined in the 1968 Geneva Convention on the High Seas and the 1982 UN Convention on the Law of the Sea. In both piracy is defined as 'any illegal acts of violence, detention or depradation committed against a ship for private ends'. The hijacking of a ship or aircraft involves taking hostages, and this is an act of violence which has been the subject of long and turgid debate in the General Assembly of the United Nations. In the Convention Against the Taking of Hostages, which was reaffirmed by a substantial majority as recently as 1985, the wording is uncomplicated and blessedly unambiguous. The taking of hostages is a criminal act, requiring states to either extradite the suspects, or if they feel that they might not be fairly treated, to prosecute. Very few suspects have been dealt with according to the Convention, despite the increasing number of incidents of hostage-taking. The reason is that few states have ratified the Convention and until that is done, they are under no obligation to follow its requirements.

In the debates that raged over the Convention a hard core of the Afro-Asian Bloc tried in vain to have hostage taking by 'national liberation movements' exempt. They were persuaded to drop their demands in return for a compromise, which even by General

Assembly standards has all the trademarks of a messy 'trade-off'. The Convention was passed, but in return national liberation fighters are now recognised by the United Nations as soldiers whose behaviour is governed by the Geneva Conventions.

One result is that hostage takers can now be tried, and if they are national liberation fighters, not as criminals, but as wayward soldiers. The pro-terrorist lobby has even managed to subvert the International Red Cross to their ends. The laws of war are applicable not just to international conflicts between states but also to 'armed conflicts in which peoples are fighting against colonial domination and alien occupation and against racist regimes in the exercise of the rights of self-determination'. This agreement dates back to 1949 when the International Red Cross, for the most genuine of humanitarian reasons tried to protect civilians from the ravages of war in all types of conflict. This was agreed by the vast majority of the 99 participating states; but it also means that captured terrorists can claim the status of prisoners of war for otherwise criminal acts. This was the price exacted to ensure the support of the majority.

The cynic would hardly find it surprising to learn that there is one Convention, passed by the General Assembly, and ratified by over half its members which has been relatively successful. In 1977 the UN adopted a Convention on the Prevention and Punishment of Crimes against Internationally Protected Persons Including Diplomatic Agents. This is a Convention initiated, created, drafted, negotiated and adopted by diplomats; who are of course its main beneficiaries. In its language it is a masterpiece. It defines those who are to be regarded as 'internationally protected people' and it makes no concessions over political motivation. The Convention requires signatory members to make *criminal* any act of violence against diplomats, their dependents and their property. Those caught are either to be extradited to the country of the diplomat or prosecuted in the local courts where the incident occurred. As an instrument of diplomacy the Convention is a model to all, as a deterrent to terrorists it has been singularly unsuccessful, as witnessed not just by the rising tide of incidents against diplomats, but that they now represent the single largest target group.

It is not difficult to be highly critical of the UN; its failures have been spectacular and we tend to ignore the success which comes from its patient day-by-day diplomacy that somehow manages to keep the lid on a dozen potential flash points around the world. It is without question the centre of international diplomacy in the world, and is as effective as its members allow it to be; so 'don't shoot the pianist – he didn't write the tune'.

Member states of the UN have prevented the organisation from enacting and enforcing international laws against terrorism, but there is no reason to believe that the battle cannot be waged effectively at the regional level. The Europeans, in response to their region having achieved the unwanted accolade of becoming the terrorist's favourite battleground, have been particularly active. In the last ten years 5000 people have been killed by the indigenous terrorists of Western Europe, while of the 200 terrorist groups known to be in existence today, at least 40 have an operational base in the capitals of the European Community.

In 1977, and in response to a terrorist offensive from an earlier generation, the 19 members of the Council of Europe discussed a Convention on the Suppression of Terrorism. The objective and the initiation by the leading members, who included Britain and West Germany, was to regard all acts of terrorism as civil crimes, and punished as such. There were to be no extradition requirements; instead every member was to bring the accused to trial before their own courts. Two member states did not sign the Convention. The Republic of Ireland's objections were predictable enough, given its own confused and violent history, and notions of an all-Ireland State. The second was Malta, which for some obscure reason is regarded as a European rather than a Middle Eastern state. On this occasion it showed its true colours, as an appendage at the time, if not a pensioner of Libya. To date, less than half of the 19 members have got round to ratifying the Convention. Amongst the 'absentees' is France, whose own capital has been under siege.

At about the same time the European Community formed the Trevi Group, named after the fountain in Rome and comprising the Ministers of Interior of the member countries. Theirs is an informal gathering, at least by EC standards and encourages greater co-operation and co-ordination over intelligence on terrorists and their organisations. The Trevi group does point to a major weakness in the battle against political violence. The terrorist has become truly international and takes no account of frontiers, but governments do, and international co-operation still leaves much to be desired. Terrorists form tight, cohesive and functionally effective alliances which are so much better organised than the responses from government.

To a marked degree, of course, it matters less whether the

Conventions are ratified. Their true importance is the political climate of co-operation and goodwill that is engendered between signatory states. This in turn leaves the way open for the police forces and counter-terrorist organisations to work together and co-ordinate their activities in the fight against terrorism.

In the last analysis, states can fight back too. Enshrined in the Charter of the United Nations is the right to self defence. In April 1986 the United States launched punitive raids against designated targets, military bases and other installations in Libya. International law regulates the use of force by states in the territory of other states. One state may not enter the territory of another without its consent, unless it is acting in self defence and even then the degree of force used must be necessary and proportionate to the threat it faces.

'By providing material support to terrorist groups which attack US citizens, Libya has engaged in armed aggression against the United States under established principles of international law, just as if he [Muammar al-Gaddafi] had used his own armed forces.' This was a clear warning, issued by President Reagan in December 1985 and in the aftermath of the terrorist attacks against Rome and Vienna airports. The Abu Nidal group was responsible and Libyan involvement confirmed in these outrages in which American citizens were numbered amongst the casualties. Whatever the political and military wisdoms of the subsequent airstrikes, there can be no questioning of the sound legal framework in which the United States sought to respond to terrorism.

15 Counter Terrorism

'If we believe a thing to be bad, and if we have a right to prevent
it, it is our duty to try to prevent it and to damn the consequences.'
Alfred, Lord Milner, 26 November 1909

Counter terrorism is a passive response to the threat of the terrorist.
In the main it is concerned with identification and prevention; with
protection, with the nullification of the effects of the sensational
terrorist outrages; but above all it is concerned with the maintenance
of law 'and order. It is conducted by skilful intelligence acquisition,
the adoption of sensible precautions, logical contingency planning
and reasoned argument, the whole being supported by an efficient
anti-terrorist capability. It is not just a governmental response. It is
an area in which the corporate enterprise and the individual all have
a part to play. Before any response machinery is put into effect there
must be an agreement and adherence to certain principles. Firstly
there must be determination. There must be an all-consuming belief
that within the democracy it is totally repugnant and wrong to be
held to ransom on issues of human rights and the principles of
freedom by a fanatical group trying to impose their minority will
through a process of terror.

To avoid anarchy the laws of the land must be upheld. There can
be no submission to pressure no matter what the price. Lebanon is a
prime example of the collapse of a country brought about by
competing factions which threw the country into a state of civil war.
To uphold the laws of the land it follows naturally that any response
must be conducted within those same laws. The targets of counter
terrorist actions and tactics must be clearly seen by the public to be
confined to terrorist organisations and there must never be the hint
that governments are using such measures as Emergency Powers
Acts to any other purpose but that for which they were intended.

Thus all functions must fall within the principles described. It is a
fact that for small numbers of terrorists to be efficient on operations
they must hold to certain military principles which are as old as the
history of clandestine forces. Secrecy is paramount to their success;
secrecy in identification and secrecy in planning. Hand in glove with
the principle of secrecy is that of surprise. If it is accepted that in
military terms surprise is defined as a state of 'unpreparedness'

126

rather than shock, it will be seen that the terrorist invariably has the advantage, as many of the counter measures to his actions are by definition overt and obvious, which gives him the planning edge. Counter measures are not immediately obvious and do not necessarily act as an immediate deterrent. Other facts too can favour the terrorist. The degree of awareness and alertness by security staff declines with time and they become increasingly bored with the routine of their work. A feeling of safety becomes pervasive, especially when there are periods between incidents. Smart uniforms aren't everything, and security staff can easily become very lax and inefficient, especially when their superiors fail to provide training programmes.

Governments usually respond quickly because once a tactic is successful it becomes popular among terrorists; for instance measures have been taken to tighten up airport security and specialist troops have been trained to take positive action against the grounded, hijacked aircraft. Options and tactics have been calculated to take care of hostage situations in strongholds such as embassies. Only in a few countries has governmental thinking progressed into planning for the yet unconducted terrorist operation. This is a weakness which the terrorist is quick to exploit by careful selection of his target, putting countries known to be merely keeping pace rather than making advances high on the list. The acquisition of intelligence is of tremendous importance to governmental counter measures and at present there is greater international co-operation than ever before. Organisations such as Interpol, the International Bomb Data Centre and other more secret official organs are being joined by informal affiliations such as the International Association of Bomb Technicians and Investigators, and other professional organisations are freely transmitting technical data to allied subscribing members.

The intelligence gathering agencies are geared towards determining the terrorist organisations' orders of battle. This in turn will assist in the identification of personalities and their different functions, information relating to future plans, evidence of involvement in past incidents and generally any information which typifies a modus operandum. Only then can clear thinking be brought to bear on the matter of counter measures. As with any intelligence operation, the counter terrorist effort runs along well practised lines. It involves a process of determining the precise requirements and the planning of the operation with clearly defined aims and objectives. The collection process ensures that only information relevant to the task in hand is passed to the next stage which is the collation process. This is the stage when all information is examined against the determined parameters, analysed and brought together to provide a full picture of the target. The final stage is perhaps where the greatest strides have been taken in international co-operation – the dissemination stage. At this point it is determined who the most beneficial users of the intelligence will be, it is usually decided on a need to know basis and it is the international spread of terrorism which has created a similar geographic dissemination of intelligence.

This acquisition trail is not easy by any means. Terrorists have been quick to learn the value of remaining small in number with well-disciplined cell structures to limit internal knowledge as much as possible. Many have been trained in Soviet schools and have learned well the lessons of the West's methods of working and the value of internal mistrust. Alongside the governmental effort is a surprisingly close co-operation between the hierachies of the major airlines; a bond which is cutting across the conventional commercial secrecies inherent in such a competitive industry. The advent of new technology as applied to security is freely debated as are other personnel-related security tactics. There are still many loopholes in the government-to-commerce relationship which could be closed in a more positive manner without the official agencies placing any of their sources in jeopardy. That day will undoubtedly come if the general principles of counter terrorism which have already been stated are to hold together.

The international sharing of information and intelligence is not without its problems. If it is accepted that the prime aim of such a system is to provide countries, persons and establishments with an early warning of likely terrorist actions and the form which they are likely to take it will be seen that the fine distinction between information and intelligence is important. In the case of intelligence which has passed the collation and evaluation point it can display a style of political thinking and assumption which may be quite offensive to the recipient and in some cases it may give an indication as to the source. The potential terrorist who is being followed and electronically targetted for eavesdropping in one country may well raise questions of human rights and privacy invasion in another country and arouse unsavoury international situations in a quite unnecessary manner.

It is possible that in the interests of national security that such an international co-operation should best be limited to information exchange on subjects of positive identification, and such details as would be helpful in the due process of law if a prosecution is to result. This mention of law raises a point which is often debated in the news media when an incident takes place, the problem of extradition.

On the face of things it would seem logical to have an agreement to the immediate extradition of all terrorists to the country in which they have perpetrated the crime. If this is considered carefully, however, it will be seen that the extradition laws in themselves can be a powerful bargaining tool in terms of delaying tactics during a terrorist/hostages negotiating operation. Far better a completely informal agreement with no publicity at all. This informality of action is a well proven course in the Western world as the 'old boy' networks, many based on Second World War contacts, continue to flourish; much to the frustration of younger officialdom and bureacracy they will probably continue to operate. They invariably cut right across the intelligence, military, political and police barriers.

Precautionary measures are noted in Chapters 20, 21 and 22, with the exception of the skymarshals which are discussed here. The principle behind the use of these men was simple. It was anticipated that under certain circumstances, a well trained and armed man could stand a perfectly good chance of taking out the hijacker in flight. This was a reasonable argument and indeed it did work on occasions on US airline flights over the United States, by the Soviet Union's Aeroflot over Russia and on board Israeli flights. The actions open to skymarshals were indeed limited; to use a firearm at altitude in conjunction with the combustibles aboard an aircraft apart from other considerations could lead to some potentially disastrous situations. The technical laboratories had a hey-day for a short time and many non-lethal weapons, sub-charged ammunition, non-lethal gases and other products of man's ingenuity came on the market. The future of the skymarshal was limited. Apart from the questionable value of his ability to operate effectively in flight it did not take long for the terrorist organisations to work out that there were only a few positions from which the man could sensibly operate within an aircraft and it became a standard operating procedure for those occupying specific seats to be searched and moved. Nonetheless for a short time at least there is no doubt that the presence of skymarshals did reduce the number of hijacks during the peak years of 1967–70 and nowhere was this more apparent than in the United States.

Contingency planning is closely allied to the intelligence acquisition effort and in this context it revolves around looking to what the terrorist organisations could do next rather than what they have done in the past. Any tactic or counter measure used in an operation has to be considered 'blown' especially if there is either press attention or an escaping terrorist and the guiding principle has to be that it will not work a second time. As there are only a limited number of permutations to any tactical puzzle this also must be kept in perspective and new tactics should not be 'blown' unless it is absolutely necessary to the success of the moment.

There is one area which is rapidly becoming almost an art form; that of hostage negotiation. This is not to be confused with the business of negotiating in a kidnap case; the ground rules are quite different. It is almost certainly the area which has benefited most from the increased amount of international co-operation. Significantly the importance of it is such that it is also the area which has benefited the most from technical research into the means of electronic acquisition of speech within the terrorist stronghold of the moment. It is a subject which lies comfortably within the sphere of counter terrorism. If the release of hostages is effected by an armed group without casualty to innocents it is a job well done, but if the release is brought about by negotiation then it is a triumph. The law has remained unsullied even in the eyes of the most left-wing journalist, innocent life has not been put at risk and the terrorists have demonstrably succumbed to the reasonable arguments of the negotiator who represents freedom and democracy.

This is not to say that the negotiating team does not need the input of the aforementioned intelligence and information. He most certainly does. There is a school of thought, and it is a perfectly logical one, which believes that the Iranian Embassy siege in London (May 1980) could have been brought to a conclusion without the loss of life had the negotiating team been armed with the full facts about the level of frustration of the terrorists. With this information the team would have been much more capable of assessing the style and timing of their moves and counter moves. This is not to detract from the magnificent job done by the police and the Special Air Service Regiment but it was perhaps an operation where the counter measures could have saved the use of the anti-terrorist 'final solution'. This would have had the twofold effect of denying certain organisations and individuals the cause to shout about 'military brutality' and could also have preserved some well-developed tactics for use on another occasion when the deployment of the military really was the last resort.

That apart, the Iranian affair had lessons for the psychologists and negotiators alike. Much reliance has been placed upon the Stockholm Syndrome – it has almost become the common pattern. In the Iranian Embassy however it did not happen. The reasons were easy to determine: within the hostage group were some fanatical supporters of the Ayatollah Khomeini, who were the equals of the terrorists in their fervour, who were willing to become martyrs themselves and indeed this was an openly expressed desire at various stages of the development of the incident. So what? It is another reason why the negotiating team need as much of the up-to-date information on the terrorists as the 'action men'. That the character of these hostages was known is beyond doubt and it may well have produced some psychological ammunition for the negotiators.

In the United Kingdom, West Germany and the USA, special forces with the armed responsibility, police and the negotiating teams train and exercise together on a reasonably regular basis and within those countries this is a fairly satisfactory situation. It is disturbing though to consider the ramifications of a truly international incident where perhaps diplomats of a number of different countries could be in a hostage situation. Is there sufficient international crossover of information, techniques and tactics and, what is more important, cross and mutual training for such an event to be catered for in a smooth and efficient manner? Should not any international conference on counter measures seriously consider this problem and put contingency planning into action to pre-empt the obvious dangers?

Probably the most debated multi-national terrorist incident to date took place on 6 September 1970. In a particularly well-planned operation Palestinian hijackers took control of two aircraft in European air space and flew them to Dawson's Field in Jordan. At the same time a third aircraft was hijacked and taken to Cairo where it was destroyed on the ground and an attempt made to seize a fourth (El Al) between London and Amsterdam. This last attempt failed due to the intervention of Israeli skymarshals who shot one of the hijackers in flight; this action also resulted in the capture of Leila Khaled (the second hijacker and also a PFLP member), who was detained in London. On 9 September, a fifth aircraft was seized. It was a BOAC VC 10 with 300 passengers, amongst whom there was a party of some 20 or so unaccompanied British school children. Leila Khaled was named as the ransom for the schoolchildren and in the face of public opinion, the then Prime Minister, Edward Heath, had little option but to agree. He held on to a condition that she would not be released until all the passengers of all the aircraft had been released, but nonetheless it was a bitter pill to swallow. This operation may have been partially successful for the PFLP but it also hardened the attitude of King Hussein of Jordan and the Palestinians were driven from the country shortly after the incident.

Fortunately the kidnapping of James Cross, the British Trade Commissioner in Canada (5 October 1970), and of Geoffrey Jackson in Montevideo (8 January 1971), followed so closely on the heels of the Dawson's Field incident that it gave the British government the opportunity to stand absolutely firm in the face of other similar release demands and so establish such a reputation for inflexibility in the face of terrorism that the country was free of such extortion incidents until the Iranian Embassy seige of 30 April 1980.

Although counter measures are largely a matter of government responsibility there is an onus also on commerce and industry to play their part in the preventive process both as a national responsibility and as demonstrable concern for the passengers who pay to be carried around the world.

It was said at the beginning of this chapter that all the counter measures have to be supported in the end by an efficient anti-terrorist capability. This is rapidly becoming a focal point for tremendous international co-operation with regard to tactics, training and specialised equipment.

Liberal democracies will always be a target for terrorism and there is little which can be done to eradicate the problem totally. Therefore the best defence is the skilful application of counter measures, a realistic education of the public and an efficient armed option, provided that it is always used as a final solution and then only within the context of the law.

16 Anti-terrorism

'Let us go and wage war
Resistance is ended;
From whom did you hear
That resistance is ended?'

'Shaka's War Song', *Long, Long, Ago,* by R. C. Samuelson

When counter-terrorism measures fail; the use of the organs of anti-terrorism are considered. This is an aggressive and potent tool of government. It principally revolves around the deployment of armed police units or military force. The very use of anti-terrorist options is a declaration of a preparedness to kill. It is one of the most emotive issues of all when considering terrorist action and government's reaction. It can lead to a situation where the rules of war are thrown out of the window and invariably commands a public examination of conscience with very good arguments for both groups in the debate to decide – 'Is it right or wrong?'

In the 'Munich Massacre' of 9 September 1972, seven terrorists of Black September assisted by a number of Europeans from various groups took over a dormitory in Olympic Village, killing 2 and seizing 9 more Israeli athletes as hostages. A number of negotiating ploys shifted the scene to Furstenfeldbrück airport when the West German police initiated a sniper attack on the terrorists. In the action which followed, 5 terrorists were killed, and one policeman and all the hostages lost their lives. The scene was the 1972 Olympics and television coverage of the incident was world wide.

Since then, the occasions when a government has directed an armed police or military response have increased. Only two years (1982/3) have passed in the intervening period when no declared government committal of armed police or troops has occurred. Even in 1982/3 it has to be accepted that it may have happened without publicity. Some of the resultant operations have been resounding successes: Entebbe, Mogadishu, the Iranian Embassy in London. It is a fact, though, that some, despite the death of terrorists, have been tragic failures due to the ensuing loss of hostage life; Munich, Larnaca, Bogotà.

Given that any such incident is as likely to end in failure as success unless the odds are firmly in favour of the assault force, begs the question, 'Under such circumstances, is it right to meet violence with violence when the lives of the hostages may be balanced in the cross-fire?' Should the executive who is imprisoned by kidnappers or sitting in a hijacked aircraft welcome or fear the intervention of specialist anti-terrorist troops?

The question as to the 'rightness' or 'wrongness' will never be answered to the complete satisfaction of everyone. It is a fact, though, that those countries which hold a special force known to be competent in anti-terrorist matters, particularly if that force has been used to good effect – West Germany, the UK, Israel, France – have been free of hostage incidents for some time now. True, the incidence of murder or bombings has not reduced and it could be said to have increased it in some countries, depending how statistics are read and interpreted. Does this beg yet another question as to whether these troops should 'go underground' in active assistance of the intelligence effort so necessary to combating the bomber?

To a degree this happens already with the SAS in Northern Ireland and the Israelis' joint endeavours between Mossad and the Sayaret Matkal; details of these operations are of course necessarily secret and so it is difficult to measure the effect. The point of view on this is tempered by the individual's personal philosophy as to what the answer to terrorism is. Can it be stamped out or reduced and if so which is the better means: sound reasoning and hence skilled negotiation or total removal, thus inviting the use of specialist military troops? It would seem logical that an argument won by negotiation has a far longer lasting effect provided that the negotiator on the side of law and order has made no concessions which weaken the status of that law. To be conquered by reason undeniably demonstrates flaws in the arguments of the terrorist which he is unable to camouflage. To kill the terrorist could produce a so-called 'martyr' to the cause and invite 'one hundred more to fill his shoes'; it could also be mooted that it hides a flaw in the arguments of the government negotiator. Within the UK the use of anti-terrorist troops is certainly viewed as a last resort and one which is brought about by the weakness of the terrorist argument, in that commitment of the troops takes place only when it is certain that a hostage death has taken place or that such a death is imminent.

It is a debate which will never be resolved as long as democracy allows free thought and free expression. Statistics are unreliable owing to the secrecy surrounding some special forces operations.

Therefore perhaps it is best to be content with a brief look at some of the organisations in existence and what they are capable of in the anti-terrorist role. With the exception perhaps of the Sayaret Matkal (Israel), whose infancy is somewhat more clouded in security, the British Special Air Service Regiment (SAS) was a forerunner in the field of anti-terrorist operations. It is important for more than just this since during recent periods of its history, it has been responsible for the training of many of the world's special forces, and it is rivalled only in its spread of influence by the Sayaret Matkal. This has naturally led to the situation where there is a commonality of training, tactics and therefore capabilities in a great number of countries. Despite this common ability, there is an important difference between the United Kingdom and those other countries outside Europe, namely the system and 'rules' by which the commitment to the military takes place; more of this later. In the context of anti-terrorism, the SAS interest began as long ago as 1969. From its post-war rebirth in Malaya in 1950, the SAS had seen very little 'peacetime' soldiering (1960–2); 1967 saw the end of the Aden campaign and the peacetime doldrums loomed once more. It was an enterprising Commanding Officer of the SAS who interested the Ministry of Defence in the prospect of the SAS instructing, on behalf of those overseas Heads of State in whose survival the country had a vested interest, suitable bodyguard teams. This was put into effect with enthusiasm and a tremendous 'educational' period was entered into in the SAS base. Assassination, kidnapping and terrorism became the subjects of intense study as teams winged their way around the world teaching the arts of protective security.

The very act of engaging in the above operations put the SAS into a good position to develop the art to a much higher degree internally and the lessons of the Munich disaster led to the instruction to create the Counter Revolutionary Warfare Wing. From 1972 onwards the SAS devoted a large part of its training effort into studying and perfecting the skills necessary for 'siege breaking'. The training scenarios were developed internally by careful analysis of terrorist motives, tactics, organisation and past incidents. Frequently interrupted by operational needs in other parts of the world, the anti-terrorist capability developed and improved. During the period between the embryo idea and 1980 which brought the Iranian Embassy siege, the SAS were stood-to on many occasions and assisted European governments frequently (Mogadishu, Assen). The latter two occasions showed to the world the previously secret agreement made in Europe for mutual assistance between countries in the face of terrorist actions.

In 1977, in the USA, SFOD-Delta was formed under the command of Colonel 'Charlie' Beckwith who had developed a taste for SAS soldiering when he had been an exchange officer with the Regiment in the early 1960s. This fact created a very close cross-fertilisation in terms of tactics, equipment and training methods (accompanied of course by a healthy rivalry); 'Delta' in itself has taught organisations outside the USA and so the commonality of purpose and capability has spread even further. Indeed there is every reason to believe that the Soviet Spetznaz conduct similar training themselves and pass this on to others albeit with a possibly different motive.

Generally speaking, such anti-terrorist units as are under discussion are drawn from the resources of an army's already extant special forces but notable exceptions are West Germany's GSG9 and France's GIGN both of which are specially trained units of the national police forces. In the USA, most states have SWAT teams within their own police forces but then the US Constitution does not allow the committal of the regular military in support of such operations within the continent.

Does the fact that an anti-terrorist unit is drawn from the police or military matter? An equal number of debaters would argue for and against. The strongest argument is that the police are the publicly recognised upholders of law and order and therefore it should be their remit. In many countries this argument holds water; in the United Kingdom there is a unique police force. It is generally unarmed and relies heavily on public trust to perform its duties efficiently. Each police officer is employed directly and individually by the Crown and has the right to partake or not to partake in an operation if he feels that it is not correct nor in the public interest as he sees his duty. They do not want the role above the point of taking care of the 'normal' armed criminal situation.

The organisation of the anti-terrorist units tends to be very similar; after all, whatever form the stronghold of the terrorist and his hostages takes it is, in effect, a box. A train, a ship, an aircraft or a building is a container. It may be made of different materials and it may be suspended in air or floating on water; whatever it is it presents the same problems to the assault force. The situation has to be contained and therefore an outer cordon has to be set up to ensure that no terrorist escapes and no one goes inside to assist him.

The prime manner of achieving this is the use of snipers and therefore a Sniper/Marksman Group is necessary.

The 'box' has to be entered (assuming that the contents cannot be forced out); there are few, if any, materials through which the modern anti-terrorist unit cannot effect entry using a variety of methods. It follows that an Entry Group is required. An Entry Group may be heavily equipped in order to carry out their task and it is natural then that a separate force is trained to pass through the portals created and this will be in the form of an Assault Group. All these Groups are assisted in their task by the input from the various Intelligence Acquisition Groups. Necessary (or at least desirable) intelligence for the anti-terrorist unit revolves around terrorist weapons; movement and placement of both terrorists and hostages and as much detail as possible on both with regard to identification in the resultant flurry of the assault. This intelligence is absolutely essential, as each snippet of information is one less factor left to chance and this is certainly a business where Lady Luck becomes the patron saint of the soldier!

Timing and surprise are key elements as they are in any military attack, and the negotiator is in a heavy position of responsibility here. In most countries, the anti-terrorist unit recognises the high degree of skill attained by the professional negotiators and never attempts to step into that position, though necessarily there is a detailed liaison between the two parties.

Many countries make a distinction between those incidents which occur on land and at sea. In the United Kingdom, a terrorist incident on the high seas and within British waters would be the responsibility of the Special Boat Service Squadron (SBS) with its Marine Counter Terrorist Team. In the USA, it would be the province of the US Navy SEAL Teams. West Germany, Italy, Malaysia and Israel, with many others, all make this professional distinction, but there are other countries which combine both, for example in Holland both land and sea incidents would be catered for by the Marines.

It would be wrong to compare in a clinical way the differences between the various units in terms of relative efficiency because so many factors, both tangible and intangible, come into play. How does the parent country assess the threat to itself and does this influence training aims and methods? The maturity of the unit itself – this is not a business which is learned overnight. The priority in the military budget – although there is a necessary core of superbly trained and motivated men – there is also a dependancy on technology especially with regard to effecting target entry. One aspect over-rides all others: experience. It cannot be taught.

What are the stresses on the men who constitute the anti-terrorist units? A soldier in a special forces unit is probably one of the most highly motivated soldiers in a nation's army; he has invariably had to push himself to the limits physically and mentally through some gruelling form of selection process and so he is fit in both these respects. He is being asked to go into a situation where the die may well be loaded against him, prepared to kill someone with whom he has no personal argument, in the defence or protection of hostages who are neither his countrymen nor his allies. Worse than this he knows that a failure will bring down the wrath and contempt of millions! In the last analysis, even though he has been ordered into the action, the due process of law will take its course afterwards and there is the chance that he could be charged with a capital crime.

There has to be a total belief in the 'rightness' of it all. The system in the UK requires the police to make every effort to resolve a terrorist hostage situation peacefully by negotiation and this they try to do with a fervour which matches that of any terrorist. In the great majority of cases, they succeed and the sighs of relief from the soldiers will invariably match those of any politician. In the event of the terrorists killing hostages or if that situation seems inevitable and imminent, the Chief Police Officer will carefully review whether or not his resources are capable of containing the incident. If he believes that the only way is to use the military, he will make that recommendation. This was the scene at the Iranian Embassy siege and it was the Prime Minister herself who acted upon the police recommendation and committed the SAS to action.

This sort of build-up to action goes a long way towards settling the soldier's conscience. He knows that every peaceful avenue has been explored. He knows that the demands being made by the terrorists are such that no democratic government could possibly accede to them. He begins the action with no doubts that it is the only solution left and thereafter instinct and years of training take over. No chances will be taken with hostage lives; their safety is paramount in his mind even to the exclusion of the safety of his comrades.

There is a clear distinction between counter and anti-terrorist measures. It can almost be classed as 'preventative' and 'curative' if it is applied on an incident-by-incident basis. Some countries do not make this distinction. Anti-terrorist forces will be committed to positive action as a result of intelligence and 'take out' the terrorists before they can conduct a planned operation or they will conduct 'retaliatory' operations after a remote event. Is this a commendable action?

Israel and the Republic of South Africa have done this regularly over the years and would defend their actions to the hilt. The USA has recently conducted one such operation and discreetly threatened another. Has it served any useful purpose? Does this tar the governments in question with the same brush as the terrorist? It has certainly created public controversy on the grand scale and it does not seem to have appreciably affected the level of terrorist incidents either on the home ground or against members of those particular countries. In interested circles it will probably fill debating agendas for years to come.

It would seem to be logical to state that regardless of how they are used, no nation can seriously afford not to have a well-trained, loyal and effective anti-terrorist unit. If that unit is properly controlled and always deployed only as a last resort and even then under close scrutiny by the law enforcement agencies then it is a force for good and undeniably effective.

Part IV

The Corporate Response

17 Corporate Awareness and Contingency Planning

Since 1970 terrorist targeting of the business world has mushroomed. It is impossible to assess either the extent or the costs involved since many corporations for the most obvious reasons are reluctant to reveal the truth. It is, however, probably more expensive to respond to terrorist threats than for example actual bomb incidents. The repeated disruptions of business and production and the shut down in operations as a result of a carefully orchestrated campaign of phone calls can cause the greater harm.

Terrorists worldwide are becoming increasingly sophisticated when it comes to waging economic warfare. They are constantly seeking new areas of business vulnerability and in societies where communications are critical, the computer has emerged as a favourite target. Especially in the developing world indigenous terrorist groups continue to hit at the support systems for modern industries. Public utilities like power lines and electricity generating stations are easy to destroy because they are so difficult to protect and defend. Defending against the more overt threats and intimidation at new construction sites and mining operations, particularly in more remote regions where government forces are ineffective and terrorists in control, is a costly business. Even the largest multinational corporations pay protection monies to some of the most obscure groups, many of which are little more than brigands with no political pretensions whatsoever.

Even in the more stable regions establishing extra physical security for sites and personnel is often easier said than done. Corporations have to rely on the quality of local skills which can prohibit the use of sophisticated equipment, and private security companies whose standards are indifferent to say the least. One answer is to transfer the risk through insurance, particularly of key members of expatriate staff. Such action is a most important point and in any case should not be undertaken lightly. If it is done properly and discreetly, insurance cover can do wonders for morale and efficiency. The better examples of insurances which provide cover for staff in the event of a kidnap are usually accompanied by security awareness training and the premium includes the services of a professional negotiator.

Like any system of course insurance is open to abuse and corruption. In countries such as Italy and Latin America, kidnap ransoms and insurance payments have evolved into a business form in their own right. Some governments believe that ransom insurance policies only encourage or stimulate kidnapping. It is the case that corporate policies do provide cover for those who are not individually wealthy, and therefore there are more potential targets than previously. In other cases it seems that the ease of transactions have reduced negotiation to a bargaining process over price and a formality which simply funds terrorism. It is for these reasons that some governments are considering a ban or prohibition of these forms of insurance. Though well-intentioned, it is our view that such laws are both impractical and counterproductive. The over-riding priority in a hostage case is to get the victim released alive and well; an objective compelling enough to find ways around legal prohibitions. The proposed laws are counter productive because it will simply drive the kidnap and ransom process underground. At present the better companies who are retained do, where feasible, involve and co-operate with the local police, and this is never an easy relationship. A ban would not only remove the police from the scene, but also deny a victim's family or corporation the resources of a trained and professionally experienced negotiator. The result can only be for ransoms to be paid quickly, and with the minimum of fuss. The word on such lucrative enterprises will spread and there will be more kidnappings and the villains will escape scot free.

Alternative strategies, especially when it comes to protecting senior executives, all have their drawbacks. The price of providing them all with armoured limousines, where a bullet-proof tyre these days can cost £3000 and more, can be prohibitive. Persuading top executives abroad to adopt a lower profile in their lifestyle is a sensible precaution and a positive contribution to reducing risk. Many, however, regard such steps as too drastic, and eliminate the benefits not only of overseas service, but also the extravagant life style which so often accompanies such service. Some executives try to adopt erratic work hours to break up any pattern and thus thwart the forward planning which goes into a kidnap operation; but this can play havoc with business and appointments have to be made often well ahead of time.

Despite these objections it is incumbent on corporations to insist on obvious self-help programmes and if necessary to compensate staff in other directions. Lower profiles are sensible and if that means the executive has to forgo the Porsche or chauffeur-driven Mercedes – then recognise the fact and compensate him with higher salaries, bonus schemes and other palliatives. Wives and dependants, who are frequently ignored, might have a few useful suggestions.

Terrorists rely heavily on inside information to carry out their operations. If a factory or facility has already been a target for terrorists it is a fair assumption that disaffected employees have had a hand in the affair. Sometimes there is little that can be done by way of preventive or corrective measures other than to monitor events. Politically motivated disaffection which is probably associated with opposition to the government or hostility towards the corporation's home base is outside the latter's competence. The terrorist for his part will adopt the well-tried and aptly-named salami tactic of subversion and infiltration, chipping away at the corporation by coercing staff to co-operate.

Even so there is much that the corporation can do to put its own house in order, and to limit the effectiveness of such subversions. Factories are often targeted because the management is unpopular. The expatriate representatives are unsympathetic to worker needs, coarse and abrasive in their behaviour which often fails to take account of local customs and standards. The West is particularly bad in this respect. The British behave as if the Empire is still in existence and the Americans insist on taking little America with them, irrespective of the havoc it causes. Both can be condescending over race and colour, and neither exerts enough control over the local management which is often brutal, corrupt and domineering in its treatment of the work force. Generalities perhaps, but in the security field corporate awareness means good staff and personnel relations. It is going to be a bold terrorist who will risk unpopularity and a loss of sympathy by targeting a factory where the employees are happy and contented under a popular management. Overseas a committed management can be as effective a form of target hardening as the latest devices in physical security.

Nevertheless, the need to operate in high risk areas will be accepted by corporations as part of the price they have to pay to remain in business. And it is in these areas of high risk that the quality of decision making by those in executive positions which is crucial to the success of the enterprise. Corporations are going to be confronted with terrorist threats. What matters is that the organisation has thought about the threat beforehand. Provision has to be made for the management of a crisis, and strategies developed and refined ahead of time, rather than after the event. Such contingency planning can address the whole spectrum of threats that can put at risk an enterprise in any country in the world. Natural disasters, storms, floods and tempests, fire (whether accidental or deliberate) will all involve pre-planning for the evacuation of staff. Component failure in procedures or manufacturing machinery, a breakdown in the supply of an essential raw material can mean expensive closedowns in operation and the laying-off of staff. At the top of the spectrum consideration needs to be given to government instabilities and regime tensions, all of which can exact an influence on enterprises both at home and overseas. Within the context of this book we will concentrate on those terrorist-inspired threats of extortion and bomb incidents.

The focal point of a contingency plan in a large corporation is the Crisis Management Committee (CMC) which is linked to overseas subsidiaries by means of mirror-image crisis decision-makers which we can call the Local Negotiating Teams (LNT). These committees, in order to be effective, need to be a permanent feature of the corporate structure, enabling them to form a healthy and positive relationship to tackle any crisis which may emerge. Contingency planning will allow them to look closely at that range of threats which affect the corporations health, well being and integrity in the future. The CMC at corporate headquarters must enjoy the complete confidence and trust of the main board, and be empowered to confront and to take as many of the foreseeable decisions as possible in advance. This will save time, economise on effort and prevent the diversion of management effort in an actual crisis.

The first stage in contingency planning is to assess the threat, in this instance from terrorists. It is a realistic assessment, based on a variety of sources which are available in-house, and from consultants. It is a constantly changing picture of threat influenced by shifting circumstances, fresh information and personalities. The Threat Assessment is based on a terrorist perception of the corporation who will have made it their business to know as much as they can about your enterprise: ensure that you are at least as well informed about them. A terrorist group planning a strike will undertake a reconnaissance of the installation, its site facilities and staff. Begin from the standpoint of security awareness and ensure that your own house is in order with regard to security precautiఒns. Target hardening in reality means being harder than other companies in the hope that the terrorist will look elsewhere for a 'softer' victim. All the potential targets are aware of this, of course, and so target hardening can easily get out of control, with competition between rivals and costs spiralling to ridiculous levels. The best approach is to study the following checklist of questions, which is by no means exhaustive, and answer them honestly.

What impression is the terrorist likely to form of your security arrangements?
How soft a target are you?
How vulnerable to attack are the critical areas in the plant?
How well are they protected?
What remedial measures can be put in hand immediately to enhance security?
How much will it cost?
How disruptive will such new measures be for business and efficiency?

Many corporations enlist the services of a specialist consultant who can undertake an objective security survey of a plant and make recommendations which are free, unbiased and noᴜ affected by corporate politics.

Having examined the physical aspects of the security a contingency plan needs to expand its horizon into the realm of grand strategy, and take in the following considerations:

What assessment is the terrorist likely to reach on the reputed wealth and financial strength of the corporation?
What are the local reactions to your corporation?
What is being said about you on television, in the newspapers?
What are local attitudes towards your country?
What are relations between your countries at the national level?

It is no longer the case that all publicity is good publicity, and it is important to be aware of what is being said about you by others. Of course, if the corporation is a bank or oil company then it does have a real problem, since terrorists are going to need an awful lot of convincing to believe you do not have unlimited wealth and resources. The answers to this second set of questions should provide the threat assessment with a view on how popular an attack on your installation would be for a terrorist group.

The next set of questions refers to the terrorist organisations:

What sort of terrorist organisation are you dealing with?
Are they linked with the criminal underworld?
What form does such an alliance take?
What are their aims and methods?
Is it publicity?
Is it political blackmail?
Is it simply money?
What types of targets will best advance these aims?
Does your corporation and its installations enhance that list?
How popular are the terrorists?
What measure of support do they receive?
   from the intelligentsia (students, teachers, journalists, universities and their professors)?
   from the media?
   from organised labour?

It may well be there is more than one terrorist group, in which case move on to the following supplementary questions:

How sophisticated and skilled do they appear to be?
Do the terrorist groups co-operate?
Is there rivalry?

Tactical considerations will take in the terrorist methods and this can best be achieved by examining the past record to answer the following questions:

What methods of attack have been most frequently, and thereby successfully employed?
Bomb attacks? If the answer is affirmative it would be helpful to learn more about such technical considerations as the method of detonation, the size and the type of the bomb and to see if a pattern to the attacks can be identified.
Bomb hoaxes?
Product pollution? This is a growing menace especially as we have already seen from the new generation of 'soft terrorists'.
Attacks on staff? Here more information is needed.

Assassination?
Coercion against local labour?
Kidnap and ransom of executives? And this question too has to be
  taken further:

> What do you know about the amount of ransoms paid?
> How long has the victim been held hostage?
> The fate of the victims, i.e. how many were killed?
> How many were released?

Contingency Planning must now take account of the support and
protection that the corporation can honestly or realistically expect
from the local police and security forces. The threat assessment
needs to know whether the corporation will be on its own. Do not
be impressed by smart uniforms, which these days seem to be the
hallmark of public and specialist counter-terrorist forces. Well-
orchestrated parades and government propaganda about their élite
formations of Green Beret, Para or SAS look alikes may be no
more than a shallow masquerade. It is an unfortunate fact that in
the developing world, many of these special forces are special only
in the size of the pay packets and the gloss on their boots and not
worthy of a second glance. It would be most unwise to count on
them in an emergency.

A good retained security consultant will probably have a special
forces background and ought to be able to answer the following
questions:

> How special are the special forces?
> How effective are the other branches and arms of service?
> Are the police efficient? Well trained?
> Is there co-operation or rivalry/friction between the police and the
>   military?
> Are they politically motivated?
> Are they popular?
> Are they corrupt?
> What do you know about the government and its judiciary?
> How effective and scrupulous is the legal system and penal code?
> Are the judges and lawyers free or intimidated?
> Are they corrupt?

All of these questions if properly researched and answered will
allow the Contingency Plan to identify the threat and where the

power lies in the country. If there is an attack the corporation will have an indication of how much support it is likely to receive and from whom. The LNT and a Security Consultant can be tasked with gathering this information and feeding the answers discreetly through to the CMC at corporate headquarters.

The membership and composition of the crisis decision makers is discussed fully in the next chapter, but before we turn to this and how a crisis may be resolved, it is important to appreciate that they will be operating under considerable emotional strain. In a real crisis they will have the responsibility for human life. In such situations the confidence and support of the board is not enough to ensure success. The CMC and its subsidiary organisations will need the very best facilities in which to operate. A control centre which is properly equipped and furnished to afford them maximum efficiency in the decision making. They will need sensible levels of support and administrative back-up and secure means of communication. We are in effect talking about a Crisis Control Centre which is secure and isolated from corporate pressure and interference.

Finally, the teams need to be practised in their role. The Contingency Plans must be put to the test and the decision-making group thoroughly exercised in their roles and duties. We advise the use of simulation games; which, though a theoretical exercise, do provide a useful means for the participants to gain experience, and if necessary be assessed in decision making under this sort of pressure.

There are in our judgement three such scenarios for simulation exercises which have immediate relevance to the needs of Corporate awareness and contingency planning. The Crisis Game, based as are the others on a variation of the MIT Simulation Model, is an international political game based upon a relevant part of the world. The exercise is designed around a crisis of mythical but realistic events and set in the near future, for example growing instabilities in a country, where the corporation is a target, or involving a plan to evacuate expatriate staff and their families.

The Kidnap Game's scenario is the ransom negotiations that involve the abduction of a corporation executive where the participants would be cast in the relevant roles and against which the contingency plan can be tested and evaluated. It could well be the corporation's intentions to train its own staff in the highly demanding tasks and particular requirements of a hostage negotiator. The Kidnap Game would help to identify those who appear to have the necessary qualities and allow them to be sent for further training and preparation.

The Product Extortion Game addresses this relatively new form of threat which has emerged. Corporations involved in food, cosmetic, pharmaceutical and medical manufacturing are particularly threatened these days. Together with the chemical industries and those involved in nuclear and fossil fuels, they have all become the target of extremist elements drawn from that broad spectrum of protest that includes environmental pressure groups and animal rights activists. It might be a simple extortion threat from a criminal gang aimed at a food company or supermarket chain. The choice of scenario can be conditioned by the threat assessment revealed in the Contingency Plan against which security procedures and responses are assessed and staff awareness enhanced.

Simulation games such as these have much of value to offer a corporation. None of them require specialist skills from the participants, and it is the writer's experience that they invariably produce stimulating debate and decision making of a high quality. It is also true that some participants find the pressures of this form of decision making uncomfortable and are unable to cope with the stress and strain involved. This is no reflection on their value to the corporation. Some executives are able to cope with business stress and take it in their stride, but when there is human life at stake, the responsibility proves too much.

It is .as well to find such things out on exercises and before the Crisis Management Team is required to operate in a real emergency.

18 Crisis Resolution

William Blundell is an executive Vice-President in an Atlanta, Georgia-based US multinational corporation. A graduate geologist, Blundell, aged 38, is a rising star in the corporation. Identified as a high-flyer early in his time at the company, he was moved out of field survey in due course and into corporate headquarters where he is being groomed for top management. For the past three months he has been in Chile on secondment to a recently-acquired copper mining subsidiary and is due to return to the US in a couple of weeks. Recently his wife joined him in Santiago leaving their children with her parents in their home town of El Paso. Yesterday morning William Blundell was kidnapped. The chauffeur-driven limousine was forced off the road and Blundell hustled out and into another vehicle. The chauffeur who witnessed the incident reported to the police that three cars and about eight men, the latter all wearing masks were involved.

In a crisis such as a kidnap and ransom which confronts a corporation, there can often be more than one casualty. The stresses and strains on senior management can for some even very experienced executives prove too much, causing mental and physical breakdown. The problems begin immediately and especially for corporations who are inexperienced. Even those with the foresight to establish a well trained Crisis Management Committee will find their initial reactions to be slow and hesitant, for the unthinkable has happened and they are reacting in a state of shock. Yet it is this initial stage which is vitally important in a hostage case, for a slow response can have an adverse effect on the chances of survival for the victim, if not the duration of his ordeal and the price of a ransom.

Corporations have top-flight security firms as consultants and there are many excellent such organisations which can assume many of the burdens, particularly for a corporation such as Bill Blundell's which is confronting such a crisis for the first time. Even so, security specialists can only advise, they cannot take those final decisions which must remain the responsibility of senior management. Thus we become witness to a potentially dangerous situation from the outset. A hesitant and uncertain corporation caught up in a crisis confrontation against a skilled, sophisticated and above all experienced terrorist organisation well versed in the hostage game. Blundell had been 'selected' by a reconnaissance and surveillance cell, lifted by an abduction group and by now was secured in a secret hideout with a guard team. In the meantime the negotiating cell, which probably includes the leader, is readying itself, while waiting in the wings will be men earmarked as a Ransom Collection Cell. There were 60 dedicated and skilled terrorists involved in the kidnap, and even as the Board's nominated CMC tries to remember its training and start to operate efficiently, William Blundell is experiencing his first night of terror.

The prime function of the CMC in Atlanta is to provide strong corporate leadership throughout this crisis. In order to make this as effective as possible, since in any case it does not take much imagination to appreciate that the odds are already stacked heavily against the corporation, the team need to be kept as small as operationally necessary to fulfil their task. Some schools of thought, when comparing the stresses which are bound to occur, maintain that the hard core of the CMC should be staffed by younger men who are less likely to buckle under the strain.

Let us begin by looking at the composition of the CMC. The chairman must be the corporation's chief executive and he needs to be shadowed by his deputy. Since both are in the normal course of events prime targets, each should have a clear grasp of how the CMC should function, and be well practised in their role and commitment. The kidnapping of Blundell is a sad and tragic affair but the crisis must not be allowed to subsume the activities of the corporation or its senior management. To this end neither the chairman nor his deputy are in permanent attendance at the CMC, their presence is only required at those critical moments when decisions have to be taken. Nevertheless they must remain in constant touch with the Crisis Centre and this might well require a co-ordinated rescheduling of their engagements.

The senior member of the hard core team we will call the Crisis Co-ordinator. Some would see this as the Director of Security but there are equally compelling reasons why this should not be the case. He has other demanding calls upon his time both within the crisis and elsewhere. In addition his work is such as to take him away from headquarters and perhaps a senior lawyer would be a good choice. He will be the Executive Secretary to the crisis, responsible for continuity and liaison with the Local Negotiating Team in Santiago, arranging the agenda of the CMC, briefing the chairman and listing the decisions that need to be taken. The CMC will need a legal specialist. Corporate liability can prove to be a minefield when the health and welfare of employees are at risk and the legal implications of decision taking will need careful consideration.

A financial adviser is necessary to arrange the ransom payment. The kidnappers are going to demand a large amount of money and this in any case is going to take a long time to organise. Payment of such an amount must be a discreet and highly confidential business, and therefore the method by which this is accounted and audited, so that the Corporation's integrity is preserved, is of paramount importance. A specialist from the Personnel and Human Affairs Department is a permanent member of the CMC to take responsibility for family affairs and staff related matters. Mrs Catherine Blundell is a formidable and headstrong lady, at present stranded in a foreign country. The children are in El Paso under the care of her parents. Her father is a recently retired Three Star Airforce General with plenty of friends in Washington.

For the moment news of the kidnap has not reached the press and media. When it does, public relations will need to be in the capable hands of a professional. As we have already seen, the media love a kidnap and this aspect will require deft control from the outset, if only because it will be an enormous advantage to have them on the side of the Corporation. The Director of Security will be required in the CMC to co-ordinate all the security needs of the Corporation worldwide. Terrorism does not recognise any national frontiers and once the word is out, there is a serious risk of other kidnaps, either by emulation or to enhance the bargaining power of the original group. Last, but by no means least, a professional negotiator must form part of the core group in the CMC where his task will be to advise on policy and techniques. At the same time another negotiator will be despatched to Santiago to work alongside the LNT.

The CMC with its core team at work will need a full administrative and logistic back-up which must include secure and independent means of communication with Santiago. Located in a self-contained complex of the corporate headquarters the CMC can work, eat and rest without intruding into corporate affairs or more importantly vice versa. They will require a small select and discreet administrative team of secretaries and watch keepers to ensure the integrity of their work. It cannot be stressed enough that attention to such details within the contingency plan will enhance the quality of decision making by eliminating some of the unnecessary burdens and encumbrances from the core team.

The CMC might well require detailed and expert advice on Santiago and the overall security/terrorist situation in Chile. Such a need would have been recognised in the earlier contingency planning and the specialists identified. They could be a recently retired senior executive who has served in Chile, a staffer at headquarters who has completed a tour or a university specialist. Such experts are not in the normal course full members of the core team but will need to be kept close by so that they can be approached and their opinion sought.

The LNT would have swung into action simultaneously. Though on a smaller scale it will mirror a number of the functions listed at corporation headquarters. Thus the head of the overseas subsidiary will chair the LNT along with his deputy, and there will be a co-ordinator and a lawyer. The security specialist will liaise with the local law enforcement agencies and pay close attention to protecting the other expatriate staff members on station. The subsidiary company in Santiago is a joint venture with a Chilean concern as is the usual practice. The latter will of course be implicated but there are probably good reasons not to allow their principals necessarily to become involved. If this is the case, the LNT should have an additional member who can act as liaison officer, smoothing ruffled feathers but keeping the locals at arm's length.

At the sharp end of the LNT is the Negotiator. Blundell has been secreted away and the initiative rests entirely with the kidnappers. It is they who will open communications, either by means of short telephoned instructions or possibly an advertisement in the newspaper. The chances are that this is going to be a protracted business, but the Negotiator will need to be by a telephone twenty-four hours a day. In situations such as these, and assuming that he is from a specialist firm of consultants, his company will rotate negotiators, probably on a thirty-day cycle.

What are the corporation's objectives? Following the precedent set by the US government there is a publicly declared policy of no concessions to ransom demands. The decision was taken by the Board and in clinical isolation of any real event. Does William Blundell's kidnap place a different complexion on policy now that his life is at stake? Perhaps in the longer term it is safer to establish the fact that the corporation is not amenable to blackmail, rejects any payment demand and is prepared if necessary to sacrifice

Blundell. Once the corporation has paid up, there is the obvious risk that its executives will become the target for other attacks, and then where is the line drawn?

It is not for the writers to sit in moral judgement, but neither is it sensible to make hard and fast rules when circumstances immediately justify breaking them and making concessions. On this occasion the chief executive instructs the CMC to negotiate for a lower ransom in the hope that by buying time Blundell's whereabouts can be discovered and a rescue effected; or the kidnappers caught when they come to collect the ransom.

Some corporations have insurance policies to cover such contingencies as kidnap and ransom in which case the whole process is taken out of their hands. In Blundell's case there is no policy (although the chairman immediately orders an investigation into such means!), so the CMC will need to examine quietly the limits it is prepared to recommend for payment. The known maximum is $60 million, again in Latin America.

At the same time there are a number of other questions which need to be addressed by the CMC and recommendations made to the Chairman for his decision. For the most part these revolve around the degree of risk the corporation is prepared to run in the light of this crisis. What are the implications of Blundell's kidnap on the corporate image, reputation and wealth? What effect will the incident have on staff morale and particularly the expatriate members overseas? If Blundell dies will there be an exodus of talent and a business loss? How good is the LNT? What confidence is there in their capabilities and how much of a free hand can they be safely given to pursue Blundell's release? Perhaps it would be better to operate directly to the Negotiator in Santiago and bypass the subsidiary except in a supportive capacity.

What should be done with Catherine Blundell? There are no hard and fast rules but it is probably better to fly her home on the first available flight. The wife (and family) is at immediate risk of a supplementary kidnap by the group to increase their bargaining power, or by others seeking emulation. If a corporate jet has delivered the Negotiator to Santiago, he will need a little while with her, and then she can return by that plane. There is a further risk that the family, whose prime objective is the release of their loved one, might easily interfere, or seek to put pressure by means of the media on the corporation. The CMC will have more than enough to deal with and do not need an emotional or neurotic spouse adding to the burden. There have been too many incidents when such ill-timed outbursts have prolonged the agony or even contributed to the death of the victim; none that we are aware of has helped to resolve the issue.

Catherine Blundell will be flown home, reunited with her children, given a safe refuge, counselled on how she can best prepare for the return of her husband and particularly how to help him to recover from the traumas of his own ordeal. This is a positive and sensitive approach which will give the family a future to plan. The corporation must have specialist counsellors, such as psychologists, who are able to help and should be in close but not obtrusive contact with the family until the crisis is resolved.

Decisions such as these ought to be circulated with the Contingency Plan and be a part of the briefing given to staff before an overseas tour of duty. William Blundell is better able to survive his ordeal if he knows that his wife has been flown home immediately and the corporate apparatus has been swung into action to safeguard his family.

Should the media and press be briefed before they hear of the incident themselves? Again, much will depend on circumstances. In Western Europe and the US there have been a number of cases where they had been taken into confidence by the authorities, and their co-operation sought and given. Where life is at risk the more responsible press can be trusted, but in William Blundell's case Latin America is bandit country. Chile is a brutal though crassly inefficient dictatorship where press censorship after a fashion is in force; so co-operation, however begrudging, could be forthcoming.

Once Blundell's story leaks out, it becomes vital to ensure that all press communiqués and statements to reporters are clear and precise. The appointed spokesman should be just that, and in this way nothing untoward is said or allowed which can undermine the chances for success.

Whilst the guidelines are being put into effect in the CMC, the negotiator will be available in Santiago to make contact with the terrorists. He could be in for a long wait; some terrorist groups, seasoned veterans in this sordid business, will delay making contact for a month or more. Whenever contact is made everything will be centred on the negotiator, his is a near total responsibility and the pressure can easily assume a dimension which is truly awesome. Psychological pressures are enormous and physical danger should not be discounted. The negotiator is a man possessed of particular qualities. In Blundell's case he will have a good local knowledge of Santiago since in negotiations with the kidnappers he will also be looking for clues which might reveal their hideout. He will know the geography, the people and speak their language. In human terms, the negotiator is bright, intelligent and alert, able to spot an opening, an opportunity however slight, which can be exploited to his advantage and bring the release of Blundell that much nearer.

There are no hard and fast rules and every hostage case needs to be judged on its own merits, but usually there are three phases to a negotiation. In *Phase One* the terrorist 'negotiator' will be coldly hostile but also calm, positive and unflustered. Telephone calls in this phase are short, sharp and very much to the point, rarely lasting longer than a minute: 'We want $X000. Do not contact us until you have it all. No time-wasting. Goodbye.'

In *Phase Two* both sides will have settled down into what could prove to be a long haul. The negotiator seeks to establish a dialogue with the terrorist. His warm and pleasant personality enables him to build a relationship, establish a rapport, even under these trying and distasteful conditions. The negotiator is a man of infinite patience, for this becomes a tactical battle, with the terrorist becoming increasingly agitated. The longer the incident lasts the greater are the chances of discovery. In a kidnap the negotiator's task is to reduce the demand from that stated – e.g. $1 million – down to an 'area of acceptability'. This is achieved by reducing their level of expectation. If the gang is experienced, and most are, the members are fully aware of the tactical moves which are open to the negotiator, as he convinces them that they have misassessed the family's or the corporation's wealth. If the gang moves too high and too fast, they must risk reducing their demands by double and even treble the amount. If the negotiator moves too low and too fast he will place the victim at risk of beatings and mutilation.

During this protracted phase the negotiator demands 'proof of life' from the kidnappers. There are a number of ways in which this can be achieved. The negotiator in his discussions with Catherine Blundell will have learned something of which only she and William are party – a favourite memory, a tune with associations, a loving nickname perhaps. This can be presented to the kidnapper as a question to which only Blundell will know the answer. Another method is to demand a photo of Blundell holding a newspaper with the headlines of a current edition clearly discernible. The problem here is that photographs as proof are dangerous. There have been cases where the victim is killed at an early stage, and deep frozen in a sitting position. He was then regularly photographed with a polaroid camera using daily papers as 'proof of life'. It would seem that questions are the best way to elicit proof of life', but it is as well to avoid dates for the victim is under considerable stress and may not remember them. On some occasions terrorists require little persuasion to oblige. Blundell could well become a pawn in the political game, with photographs and even videos released to the press in which Blundell, the 'symbol of a capitalist oppressor' becomes an empassioned plea for release and a hard denunciation of the Chilean regime.

The negotiator needs very precise instructions at every stage of the process. Though he has full responsibility he does not have authority to make or take decisions. He cannot be in a position to grant the kidnapper's demands. Throughout, the response will always be something along the following lines: 'I understand what you are saying but you must understand my position. I have no authority to agree to your demands, so let me see what I can do and I will discuss it with you the next time we talk.'

Eventually, and this can sometimes be months away, the negotiation enters the *Third and Final Phase*. If all has gone according to plan, the negotiator will have come increasingly to dominate the negotiations both over the size of the ransom and on the means of delivery. Possibly the police through their own intelligence network and resources have been able to build a fairly clear and accurate picture of whom they are up against. The question of the role of the police and law enforcement agencies is complex. In Blundell's case the police have been involved from the outset because of the public manner of his abduction. In other instances where there is an effective Contingency Plan in existence much will be known of police reliability and efficiency. Even in Blundell's affair they need not be fully involved if there are any doubts about their capabilities. Their representative can be invited to attend only specific sessions held by the LNT. It is worth remembering that the police, whilst anxious to secure the safe release of William Blundell, also have other objectives, not least the destruction of the terrorists. Petty jealousies, rivalries and personalities can easily intrude, while interservice rivalries between police and army can jeopardise the operation.

Assembling the ransom will take time. The terrorists have demanded $5 million in small denomination notes. Even so the bank note numbers need to be recorded and thus police and bank co-operation is essential. A ransom of this size is bulky. Packaged in $10 bills it weighs close to a thousand pounds. It will take time to raise the money and it has to be secured until a delivery is agreed. Volunteers will be needed to deliver the ransom; they should be two men.

It has yet to be ascertained whether a ransom payment is legal under Chilean law. In some countries it is prohibited, and this means that the payment has to be arranged in a third country, or police co-operation sought in the hope that the ransom payment can be seen in part as a means of flushing out the terrorists. Payment could be attempted by means of a careful subterfuge but such a course of action is fraught with risk. Everybody involved from the company is under police scrutiny and surveillance. The corporation will also wish to continue its operation in the country. Terrorist ransom demands invariably include money but this need not be exclusively the case. Kidnappings that are primarily political in purpose can present a more complicated picture. Specific terrorist demands can involve the release of imprisoned comrades and this automatically brings governments into play. The CMC in Atlanta would then be dealing with Washington and Santiago as well as the terrorists through their own LNT. Political kidnappers want publicity, to inspire fear, demonstrate government incompetence and win adherents to the cause. A case in Italy involved the kidnapping of a wealthy industrial magnate whose ransom was a rent rebate for the poor of Naples. Sometimes the achievement of political objectives is victory enough and the hostage becomes 'surplus to terrorist requirements'. The Italian politician Aldo Moro was brutally slaughtered when he was no longer of any use to the terrorists.

Inter-government involvement elevates the crisis and unless the corporation is particularly bold, imaginative and determined it will lose out to the machinations of international diplomacy. The whole affair becomes public, with all the attendant problems of the media hype, where all the world is reading everybody else's mail, and William Blundell becomes an expendable pawn in a power game. In such an instance the corporation must not lose sight of its objective. It wants William Blundell home in the shortest possible time for the least amount of ransom and in a fit enough mental and physical state to resume his work and realise his profit-making potential. This is a tall order and the corporation may need to mobilise its influence on Capitol Hill, including Blundell's father-in-law!

Does William Blundell return home to Catherine and the family in El Paso? Statistics show that his chances at best are evens. Whether he is able to resume his work and realise his potential is a mark of the man, his character and resilience to overcome a terrible ordeal.

19 Diplomats and Terrorists

'We only need to be lucky once, you need to be lucky always.'

PIRA, October 1984

In recent years diplomats have been singled out for terrorist attacks specifically because of who they are, the positions they hold and the functions they perform. In the years after 1967 and in the wake of the June War which radically altered the balance of power in the Middle East, terrorism became an even greater menace. Since that time there has been a five-fold increase in the incidence of attacks on diplomats. Representatives of 112 countries have suffered in this fashion.

In April 1983 a suicide bomber from Islamic Jihad attacked the US Embassy in Beirut, an event which was just another statistic in an upward trend. The US State Department in its statistical overview of terrorist incidents involving diplomats and embassies has published other, and equally sobering, statistics. Twenty ambassadors from 14 countries have been assassinated and diplomats from a further 43 countries have been kidnapped. Nor is it surprising to learn that since the Tehran mob stormed the American Embassy and held the staff hostage, the incidence of embassy seizure by terrorist groups and illegal political parties has increased dramatically. The embassies of 45 countries have been seized in a total of 75 attacks and this represents a 50 per cent increase since Tehran. In another report the State Department's Office for Combating Terrorism has estimated in its study, 'Terrorist Incidents Involving Diplomats', that such attacks, which in 1975 accounted for 30 per cent of all terrorist incidents, had jumped to 54 per cent a decade later.

Today the diplomat is the most popular of terrorist targets, and it is not difficult to see why this should be the case. The primary aim of the terrorist is extensive publicity and an outrage against the diplomatic community serves those needs perfectly. Attacking a diplomat blatantly violates the principles and conventions of diplomatic immunity, causes concern to their community and provokes an immediate crisis for governments. Diplomatic immunity is based on custom and on traditions which have become conventions, and on international law; some of which we have already discussed.

The list of regulations governing just this aspect of behaviour between the States is impressive.

The Vienna Convention on Diplomatic Relations
The Vienna Convention on Consular Relations
The Convention on the Privileges and Immunities of the United Nations
The Convention on the Prevention and Punishment of Crimes Against Internationally Protected Persons Including Diplomatic Agents

Where did it all start? Taking hostages, of course, is an age-old custom which can be traced back to the earliest times when tribal leaders would hold the children of another and subject tribe to ensure the latter's good behaviour. Immunity for representatives is almost as old, and enshrined in military ritual from the battlefields of the past which allowed safe conduct.

For the origins of diplomatic immunity in the sense we would use the term today, one finds it in English history, in the reign of Queen Anne. It is here that we find the first recorded incident which placed diplomats beyond the reach of civil law, and helps explain why these days they cannot be fined for speeding, or fined for illegal parking. The Ambassador Extraordinary of the Tzar of All the Russias had on a number of occasions been taken from his coach by thugs hired by his creditors and thrown into Newgate prison for non-payment of debts. Upon the third occasion when such indignities were heaped upon His Excellency, the Crown enacted a law through Parliament. (Russian goodwill was important to English interests in the timber trade in the Baltic where England was having a few problems with the Swedes at the time.) This law declared that anyone implicated in serving a writ or process against an ambassador or other envoy or his domestic servants was a 'violator of the law of Nations and disturber of the public peace', and punishable as such.

Diplomatic immunity from criminal law is even older. During the long reign of the Protestant Elizabeth I the ambassadors of their Catholic Majesties, the Kings of France and Spain, plotted her downfall and death. Their successors got up to similar antics during the Commonwealth period of Oliver Cromwell a half century later. The plots were discovered by the English 'secret service' of the day and the ambassadors were exposed. The ambassadors, though caught committing acts of treason, were merely sent home. Their English co-conspirators were not so fortunate – they headed straight for the block, by way of a few unspeakable nasties in the Tower of London en route.

The practice of diplomatic immunity has endured a very long time and survived in the face of major if not revolutionary changes to the international system. Any custom or convention which has survived in the face of such odds must indeed be highly prized. Its value lies in the principle of its *reciprocity*. A state grants immunity to the representatives of another country, and suffers the inconvenience which that implies, so that its own agents abroad may receive the same concessions and freedoms.

Diplomats are a privileged caste, outside the laws of the land, and this is because they represent their country, but are not responsible for its actions. What was so horrific in the Tehran Embassy incident, and potentially so destabilising for international peace and stability, was that the American diplomats were adjudged accountable for US policies. The manner of their seizure and imprisonment was an act which elevated terrorism into the higher levels of interstate relations. These days terrorists show scant respect for diplomatic immunity and if diplomats are no longer respected because of their status, they have to look for other means for their protection.

In London this is the task of the Royal and Diplomatic Protection Group, part of the Metropolitan Police, who are supported when the occasion demands by the security services and that élite counter terrorist unit, the Special Air Service Regiment. Theirs is a formidable if not impossible task. There are at present accredited representatives from 135 states in London. This means that there are over 5000 diplomats which, with their families, comes to about 20 000 people to be protected. The police also have to watch over 460 buildings belonging to the diplomatic community. In New York, which houses the United Nations, and Washington, which is the diplomatic capital of the world, the numbers of people and buildings demanding protection are even higher. Statistics aside, however, the diplomat and his embassy present security forces with a number of problems which are unique; they are not encountered in the commercial world.

Embassies usually occupy the oldest and most prestigious buildings in the capital, especially in the Western world. The buildings are old, often listed because of their architectural significance, and protected by laws which prevent their modification to meet the needs of protection and defence. Security measures can be enhanced, provided that the fabric is sustained, the façade maintained and the overall 'architectural ambience' preserved. There are few occasions where the opportunity is presented to build from new, as with the United States embassy in Grosvenor Square, London, with its fortress-like appearance; or when a government decides to resite the whole diplomatic community, as in the case of Britain, which moved its Saudi Arabia embassy from Jeddah to Riyadh.

Embassies try to project an image of welcome and freedom to their thousands of visitors, and they are anxious to promote their country, and to encourage tourism and business. This runs counter to the needs of high security which can present a picture of oppression and restrictions; of cameras and locked doors, of passes and armed guards. Arab and Muslim countries have a culture where the emphasis is on hospitality and the 'open door' and these needs present security specialists with major headaches. Diplomats have to rely on the quality, in terms of courage and efficiency, of the local forces for their protection. In London these forces enjoy a high reputation, but elsewhere in the world standards vary enormously as does the level of threat. In recent years most terrorist incidents against diplomats have taken place in Western Europe. This is not necessarily a reflection of the quality provided but instead that unique combination of factors which make Europe an attractive target for terrorist activity, not least because of its geographical convenience to the Middle East.

Terrorist attacks against diplomats can take several forms. Kidnappings, hostage seizures, bombings, hijacks and armed attacks have all been attempted. Bombing appears to be the preferred method for all the reasons we have discussed, and at present accounts for about half of all recorded or reported incidents.

In the previous chapter we looked at crisis resolution in the form of a corporate kidnapping. In the case of diplomats the process is immensely more complicated because there are political issues at stake. Diplomats are rarely taken hostage for a financial reward alone, would that it was that straightforward. When ambassadors or diplomats are kidnapped abroad, many of their parent governments have a declared policy of no negotiations let alone concessions to terrorist demands. Consequently kidnapping or 'diplonapping' as the Americans call it, in the traditional sense, has declined, and cases such as Geoffrey Jackson's have become the exception in recent years.

Diplomats are also involved when aircraft are hijacked. The aircraft are invariably those of state airlines, and the incident is international by its nature, while the terrorist will invariably have political demands to exchange for his hostages. It is a complicated affair, as witnessed by the Air France Boeing 737 which was hijacked by Islamic Jihad, whose demand included the release of fellow members of this fanatical organisation who were either under sentence of death or serving long prison terms in Kuwait for a previous hijacking. States are as loath to agree to the release of terrorist prisoners in response to a blackmail as they are to grant asylum which is a requirement of the hijackers. This form of terrorist blackmail is a very real threat and an increasingly potent weapon in the hands of ruthless and fanatical groups. The threat is enhanced because so many states seem unable to cope with such incidents, be they hijacks or embassy seizures. They possess neither the resources nor the means to succeed in these difficult situations, either through the use of skilled and experienced negotiators or professionally competent anti-terrorist forces. All too often hijacks go wrong, as witnessed by the Egypt Air hijack in Malta and more recently the Pan-Am incident at Karachi.

Governments have a duty to protect the lives and property of aliens resident in their country and this is especially true in the case of diplomats. The USA is particularly tough, especially when it comes to cases of kidnap. Given its own history of well-publicised incidents (the Lindberg case, etc.), kidnapping of diplomats is a felony or a federal offence, involving Washington rather than local or state authorities. One of the principal aims of terrorist attacks against diplomats is to demonstrate the weakness, incapacity or unwillingness of a host government to discharge its obligations and responsibilities. It is precisely because of their special status that terrorists single out diplomats as favoured targets. It is hardly surprising therefore that such incidents, with all their attendant media hype, cause a major crisis for any government. In some instances, a government, particularly some of those in the developing world, can close in on itself and adopt a siege mentality. Decisions are then made by the head of state and a few close advisers – the key figures would probably be the Ministers of Interior and Defence, together with chiefs of staff of the armed forces. Though diplomacy is involved and foreign relations are affected, it is not usual to find the Foreign Minister included within the circle of decision makers. Foreign Ministers tend to be respected figures, professionals in the diplomatic world, but rarely part of the inner sanctum and thus in crises of this nature, sidelined. Perhaps one reason for this is that on tough issues like terrorist hostage-taking, political survival and regime prestige take precedent over foreign relations.

It is also much easier for those who have a mind to do so to assess the performance of a government in both the outcome and the manner in which it handles a situation. This explains why some governments may decide to cut off the terrorists, bury the crisis by means of a blanket of prohibition and blackout the media, thereby retaining control over the conduct of affairs.

Despite public statements to the contrary, governments have to talk to terrorists, particularly in hostage incidents. In a stated policy of no concessions, communications, let alone negotiations, can be interpreted as a sign of weakness which elevates the terrorist to an equal status, so elaborate ways around this have to be found. Intermediaries are used in a complicated process of dialogue which can also involve another government as well as the terrorists themselves. Perhaps that is why Britain and France, together with those who appeared to have responsibility for such issues within the Reagan Administration, were prepared to leave negotiations for the release of their people (some of whom have diplomatic status) held by Islamic Jihad in the hands of Terry Waite. This envoy negotiated with the terrorists directly as well as with representatives of the Syrian and Iranian governments. For a while this tactic was successful but when Waite attempted further negotiations, and in the face of earlier revelations of 'Irangate', he became a hostage himself.

In the event of a hostage incident involving its diplomats abroad, most governments would mobilise their own Crisis Management Committees to monitor the incident; such a committee is similar to that of the corporate sector in its structure and organisation. Thus the chairman of the CMC could well be the Foreign Minister or his Deputy, who would head a small tightly knit group operationally capable of responding to the crisis. The risk is that where bureaucracy is concerned such organisations can easily become top heavy and unwieldy which can not only adversely affect the crisis, but subsume the workings of the entire Ministry. The Embassy in the country where the incident occurred should also establish its own LNT to handle the situation on the ground.

The Rand Corporation's Think Tank on Anti Terrorism has identified five principal types of terrorist activities directed towards incidents involving diplomats. Their director, Brian Jenkins, listed them as follows:[1]

Those associated with guerrilla warfare – insurgence or on-going terrorist activity.

Those by ethnic emigré or exile groups against a particular nation or régime.

Worldwide attacks by terrorists abroad as part of a larger campaign against a specific government.

Those by indigeneous groups to protect the actions of a foreign government.

Government use of terrorist tactics or groups in a surrogate warfare against a foreign foe.

This last area in Brian Jenkins' catalogue takes us into that murky world where diplomats have a point of contact with terrorists. We have looked at the diplomat as victim, but it is frequently the case that many incidents of terrorism could not have occurred without diplomatic support. Iraq was a major offender until it became embroiled in the Gulf War and suddenly found that it needed friends in the Western world. In April 1984, staff in the Libyan People's Bureau in London behaved more like street hoodlums than accredited representatives, when they opened fire on a peaceful demonstration and WPC Yvonne Fletcher was gunned down. In October 1986 the Syrian Embassy in London was caught with its 'finger in the till'. The Ambassador and other senior members of his staff were implicated, and named in a British court as accessories to an attempt to blow up an El Al jumbo jet. Their plaintive denials and counter claim that they had been framed by Israel's Mossad defied belief. One can assume that more discreet evidence could readily be furnished to governments seeking solid proof of Syrian duplicity, from the surveillance undertaken by British intelligence services.

In the face of such a blatant contravention of diplomatic protocol and privileges, Britain had no alternative other than to sever relations with Syria. The pity and the shame is that when London looked to its European partners for support and collective action that proved singularly unforthcoming. The Greeks remain the odd man out when dealing with terrorism, but the French position is hard to fathom given the barrage of bombs which have exploded in Paris. Syria may be a de facto power in the Middle East, and a key to the French predicaments in the Lebanon, but an appeasement of terrorism can never be the answer. There is nevertheless increasing concern expressed by many states over the lawful conduct of foreign missions on their territory. Embassies, missions and residences are inviolate. Police cannot enter these buildings even if they believe a crime has been committed or terrorists are hiding. Diplomatic bags cannot be opened or searched. This is essential of course for confidential communications between missions and governments, but diplomatic bags have also been used for smuggling firearms, explosives and peoples.

The abuse of diplomatic privilege is rapidly becoming the norm rather than the exception and the need to review the conventions which make this possible is obvious and pressing. Any such review however is bound to be a long and complicated process given the only areas in which it could be held, which is the United Nations. Such a turgid forum of debate will provide ample opportunities for those friends of the terrorists to procrastinate and delay. Reform will be even further away and in the meantime the system will be broken and abused in the most cynical fashion by states who sponsor terrorism.

Of course, while diplomats may look forward to many years of immunity and privilege, this has never been the case for their masters, the heads of state. For them the threat of the assassin, with gun or bomb, has become very real. The following extract from *The Times*, compiled in 1984, is testimony of the efficacy of the terrorist.

THEY DIED IN POWER
THE ASSASSINS' TOLL OF WORLD LEADERS[2]

August 1949: Hosni Zaim, President of Syria, shot by the Army

July 1951: King Abdullah of Jordan, assassinated in Jerusalem

July 1958: King Faisal of Iraq, killed in military coup

September 1961: Rafael Trujillo, dictator of the Dominican Republic, assassinated

November 1963: President John Kennedy, assassinated in Dallas, Texas

January 1965: The Prime Minister of Iran, Hassan Ali Mansour, shot dead

January 1966: Abubakar Tafawar Balewa, Federal Prime Minister of Nigeria, died in coup

September 1966: The South African Prime Minister, Hendrik Verwoerd, was stabbed to death

March 1975: President Ngarta Tombalbaye, died from wounds received when the Army overthrew his government in Chad

August 1975: Sheikh Mujibur Rahman, President of Bangladesh, died in shooting in his Dacca home in an army coup

February 1976: General Murtala Muhammad, Nigerian head of state, shot dead in an unsuccessful coup

April 1978: President Muhammad Daoud of Afghanistan, killed in coup

June 1978: Lieutenant-Colonel Ahmed Husain al-Ghashmi, the Yemen Arab Republic president, killed by parcel bomb

October 1979: President Park Chung Hee of South Korea, shot and killed

April 1980: President William Tolbert of Liberia, shot dead in a military coup

May 1981: Zia ur-Rahman, President of Bangladesh, shot by group of rebel army officers

August 1981: Iranian President Muhammad Ali Rajai and the Prime Minister, Muhammad Javad Bahonar, killed in a bomb blast in Tehran

October 1981: President Anwar Sadat of Egypt, assassinated by soldiers

September 1982: Bashir Gemayel, President-elect of Lebanon, killed in bomb blast

October 1984: Mrs Indira Gandhi, Prime Minister of India, assassinated by members of her own bodyguard in the grounds of her Residence.

In October 1984 the PIRA tried and failed to kill the British Prime Minister. It is their chilling words which head this chapter. And in February 1985 Olof Palme, Prime Minister of Sweden, was shot down by an unknown gunman in a Stockholm street.

NOTES

1. Brian M. Jenkins, *Terrorism and Personal Protection* (London: Butterworth, 1985).
2. *The Times*, 1 November 1984.

Part V

Protecting the Individual

20 Target Hardening

Up until about ten years ago, the term 'target hardening' was usually applied to the measures taken to prevent arms and explosives falling to terrorist hands as well as to those physical measures taken in target denial. It has now been extended into a more personal application as individuals have in themselves become prime targets on a scale well outside the normal diplomatic circles. It is almost a prophylactic process and by inference concerned with barriers. However, these barriers are not all physical, and in this chapter we discuss the 'barrier' most pertinent to the individual. The denial of means through the application of commonsense rules. Full 'denial of means' is not possible but the term is a good one to have in mind as it expresses quite clearly the intention of denying the terrorist the opportunity to strike with ease. In tandem with this denial of means comes the adoption of sensible procedures and basic security devices and aids. We are only concerned with the individual in this chapter, though many of the rules outlined can usefully be applied within the corporate body. This is not a technical section; provided that the individual wishes to live and work in a secure atmosphere, then the application of a set of simple procedures will do far more towards the well-being of himself and his family than any number of sophisticated devices. The keywords to sound individual security are:

Awareness
Observation
Planning
Reaction

In themselves these are obvious and need no discussion; if they are all applied in the areas outlined, then the individual is a long way towards becoming a 'hard target'.

The well-trained executive can cope with minor criminal attacks such as mugging, but in the face of a concerted terrorist action or kidnap manoeuvre he is unlikely to do anything other than increase the risk of personal injury. If this is accepted as a fair statement of fact then it is sensible to attempt to reduce the likelihood of such violent episodes by applying the 'keywords' to some general principles and procedures. Adopt the four Ps:

Profile
Planning
Predictability
Practice

Profile.   Do not unnecessarily advertise your personal or corporate wealth. As mentioned earlier in the book, kidnaps are now taking place in countries like Peru and Colombia where the sole invitation is the lure of dress, jewellery and the expensive briefcase. Be circumspect in hotel bars in declaring either wealth or type of business. Today's 'lounge lizard' is not on the lookout for unattached females; he is target hunting with a totally different purpose. Travel and live overseas with a simple, believable cover story.

Planning.   Different aspects and occasions which need detailed planning are covered later but, in general terms, have basic contingency plans for all eventualities. Escape routes, consulate contacts, police and emergency services should be on your rapid checklist wherever you find yourself.

Predictability.   Routines are deadly! It is possible to vary them with a little imagination. It is surprising, with the wisdom of hindsight, how many kidnap victims can recall the warning signs which should have alerted them. Do not fall into the trap of varying timings and routes to a pattern that in itself becomes predictable. If you are a worthwhile target, the reconnaissance phase can take months!

Practice.   This is an essential ingredient to the executive who employs personal staff at the office, at home or uses a chauffeur. Most staff respond to this with a real will – in effect it also enhances their security. Where it is possible to practise a contingency plan, do so, it is excellent insurance.

Before going into detail, there are some other areas of a general nature which should be amongst the considerations for security. Military principles of in depth defence hold equally true for the executive at home and in the office. Adopt the inner sanctum mentality at the same time maintaining escape routes should this become necessary. Do not base your defence on one outer cordon such as alarms, reception staff, guards or armour plating. From within the inner sanctum and preferably before moving into it, there should be the ability to call upon the police or other assistance.

Ensuring that this is always possible invariably requires the use of radio-telephones, especially in the car.

No matter how proud you are of your own security measures, never discuss them with persons who do not need to know: a secret shared is a secret halved. It is a good idea to record all emergency numbers in a small security envelope to be lodged at the office, home and to carry with you. Log blood groups, medications, etc., of all members of staff and family about whom there is concern. Once you have determined upon your personal security plan, subject it to scrutiny and practice; if it works then have confidence in it. Remember to carry out regular reviews. This serves three major purposes. Firstly, it refreshes you and your staff on the reasons for them. Secondly, it will show up the areas where human laxity has begun to have an effect and thirdly, it gives you the opportunity to consider the plan against changes of circumstance or an increase in the threat level.

Chapters 21 and 22 examine more closely the problems of security at home and in the office. Here the concern is with those areas which can be shown statistically as being occasions when the target is most vulnerable to assassination or kidnap. It is a fact that the highest incidence of cases take place when the target is in a car or embarking/disembarking from it. This makes perfect sense, for it is generally whilst engaged in these routines that the target can most easily be observed, recorded or shot at.

It is usually at these times that he presents the clearest and most predictable target to the sniper and it is relatively easy to ambush the unwary driver, provided that his route can be predicted. President de Gaulle of France, himself a survivor of at least thirty assassination attempts, solved the problem by employing a security service of a few hundred people; a multitude of armoured vehicles and at least one 'double'. We have made the assumption that, at the most, our diplomat or executive will have a chauffeur. It makes sense to look at the vehicle first. Some readers will have or be contemplating having their car up-armoured. Some will never be in that position. Whether it is a basic car or an armoured version, there are two important areas for consideration. There are on the road incidents and off the road. The latter is the simplest to deal with and so it is discussed first.

The basic premise is that when not in use the car will be locked and within a secure area; a garage, corporate parking lot or the like, and this of course gives a degree of protection. Consider however the flexibility which the modern bomber has at his fingertips. It is the work of seconds to place a magnetic (limpet) type bomb to the underside of a car to be operated by a vibration or trembler initiation switch; he is well away by the time the bomb actually explodes.

In the longer term if the vehicle has been left unattended for a significant time and especially if it was a predictable action to park the car which could have been ascertained by an observation team, e.g. regular business trips requiring the car to be left at an airport for a couple of days or so; then the bomber can, and frequently has, given free range to his ingenuity and the technical advances of his craft. The main point here is the predictability of the parking session which will allow the bomber to accurately decide how much time he has 'on target'. A skilled operator does not need more than half an hour or so to fit the most complex bomb and very effective ones can be fitted in minutes. Devices themselves can be made to look like a variety of component parts which could fool the casual inspection. A smear of grease and road dirt and they can appear as though they have been there for years.

Any car has certain elemental parts and functions which lend themselves to bomb initiation. There is electrical power to an abundant number of strategic points; heat is present in a number of places to a calculable level; gas pressure is available and again to a calculable level. There is movement; there is vibration; and there is pressure under wheels, seats and floor carpets. Driver actions are predictable; lights will be turned on; indicators will be used, sharp turns will be made and bumps in the road will be encountered. All these and many more can become the point or means of initiation for a bomb.

There are many devices on the market now which act as standing security. The basic systems when fitted to a car will, through an integral transmitter, give visual and/or aural warning to a small pocket-carried receiver. They are not 100 per cent proof against false alarms but they are a useful tool for casual parking, visits to the theatre or restaurants. These have their place in security planning, but at the end of the day any person at risk needs to be able to search his vehicle competently and safely.

You will need a good quality torch which does not have to be large, and a mirror is of assistance. If you know your car (and that after all is the first essential), a dental mirror is adequate if you wish to carry the equipment in your briefcase. The first step is obvious: a thorough external check. Examine wheels, wheel arches and all natural ledges and tunnels such as exhaust and housing, shock absorbers, etc., look for anything unnatural and accept that you may get dirty. As you open the first door – release it to the first catch and check both visually and VERY GENTLY with something like a credit card for attachments or the like. It makes sense to start with any door except the driver's. Look around without entering and examine under the dash; door pockets; seats; and carpets. Open other doors in the same manner, regardless of the fact that you have already looked inside. Release the bonnet and hold the pressure until you have checked all round it – continue to observe for attachments as you lift it slowly. Make a thorough inspection of the engine compartment, looking in particular for component parts which 'don't seem right' and for clean wiring. Carry out the same procedure with the boot. Remember spare wheel and tool box compartments.

Finally, double check the driver's seat, door pockets, glove compartments, sun visors and ashtrays, being careful to adopt the same procedures with any compartment which has a door or similar cover. If you find anything at all unusual, get expert help – do not attempt to dismantle any device yourself. If someone has gone to the trouble to place a professional device it is quite probable that there will be some form of anti-handling device. The armouring of vehicles is a complex and detailed business. Suffice it to say here that only the most reputable companies should be engaged. Remember what was said about in-depth defence; an armoured car with all its virtues is only a small part of the overall security plan.

There are modifications to the normal executive car which can be carried out relatively inexpensively and which can greatly enhance the security of the occupant. High speed and mobility play a great part in evasive tactics and therefore look towards achieving this first. Run flat tyres (i.e. those which allow the vehicle to be driven even when punctured or deflated) are an essential, and also consider fitting a self-sealing petrol tank filled with 'explosafe', which is a fine steel, expanded mesh, fitted within the tank which prevents an explosion; it has only a minor effect in reducing tank capacity. Fit inertia-reel seat belts to all seats and install an internally-operated electrical door-locking system. The fitting of quartz-halogen spot lights front and rear aimed at driver height can be a useful aid to getting out of trouble at night. There are occasions when the car may have to be driven offensively; therefore fit steel bars to the front and rear behind the conventional fenders. Internally adjusted door mirrors, good security locks to the boot, petrol cap and bonnet are a good preventive measure but do not rely on them. A loud siren can often bring police assistance to you and in itself it may discourage your being followed. Lastly, remembering the earlier point on communications, fit a radio telephone.

Before discussing some on-the-road tips, it is important to recognise three things; apart from forming an integral section of your security plan, your car on occasions can be used in the manner of an offensive or defensive weapon. If you accept this, then you should accept that training in handling that weapon will stand you or your chauffeur in good stead. It is available from expert commercial companies. Lastly, maintenance, as with any weapon, is vital. It is also a risk. Select your garage carefully, register for servicing under another name (pay cash) and remove any security device before the car goes in for servicing and search it most diligently when it returns.

Let us now turn to the hazards of actual driving. First in priority has to be careful route selection and planning. All your routes must be recorded with hazard points marked and coded. Include on this map areas of radio screening. Try to select routes with a minimum number of natural ambush sites and if possible try to have one or two 'safe' houses en route: police stations or highly public areas to which you can drive with headlights ablaze and siren screaming if necessary. Have simple location codes for progress points along each route which can be signalled into home or office whilst you are journeying between. If this system is to be used, it must be used effectively – that is, if you are late in calling up or arriving then the contingency plan must be put into action. Better the occasional false alarm than disaster. The maps must be cared for with as much diligence and discretion as any confidential document.

If you are driving in a high threat area, the golden rule is to regard every other road user as a terrorist or criminal out to get you. In simple terms this means that many of the normal driving functions become exaggerated. Mirrors should be in constant use (if you are chauffeur-driven, make sure you have your own separate mirror), keep to the fast or middle lanes wherever possible, drive in convoy on those occasions where it may be possible to go to work with your colleagues and allow constant manoeuvring space between cars, regardless of speed. If you do not trust a situation ahead of you, U-turn out of it immediately. Accidents and broken laws can be argued with the police at a later stage. If you suspect you are being followed, it may be for a reconnaissance or for a hit. A hit will usually require four passengers and possibly two cars. Take no chances: get as full a description as possible; make a few manoeuvres to ensure that the tail is positive, and radio the details in as a precaution. If danger looks imminent head for one of your safe houses in the manner described earlier.

Statistically, the most used ambush site for the assassin or the would-be kidnapper is the home of the victim. Some fairly inexpensive security equipment and the following of some simple rules make the criminals' task very difficult (especially if your car is armoured). Radio controlled gates and doors are essential. It is ridiculous for a VIP in this day and age to have to get out of his car, or indeed to stop the car outside his home. Drive the last few hundred yards with headlights and spot lights to assist a cursory search. The action of remotely controlled gates or doors should also trigger floodlights. Drive into your garage and remain locked in the car with the engine running until doors and gates have closed behind you. It should go without saying that access to the house must not necessitate you going outside the garage again.

There are many other classic ambush sites: the natural ones are obviously any sparsely populated area where either terrain or traffic control systems force you to slow down or stop. The dangers of these can be reduced by careful route selection and regular switches. There are some commonly contrived situations, however, which would bear to be briefly mentioned. First there are road blocks by hostile cars. These cars themselves are usually sited for quick getaway and are thus parked at an angle to the road. If it is out of the question to do a 'bootlegger' turn, which is a technique of using the handbrake and a violent transference of the car's weight from one side to the other in order to effect a high speed change of direction, or simply to reverse, then ram the lightest end of the cars (usually the boot) and drive on using spotlights and sirens to the nearest safe haven.

Falsely constructed road works are a traditional means of ambush. If any suspicious diversions occur, then change routes immediately. It is as well to be aware of the normal style of roadworks and diversion signs in a strange country; study how they are normally laid out, as improper signs are a definite cause for suspicion. False police and military checkpoints are another hazard. Some countries allow these to be conducted in plain clothes but although you may be stopped, do not get out of the car, keep the doors locked, and stay in gear with the engine running. If you become suspicious, drive through and report to the nearest police station. Accidents are often faked. Obey the drills and stay locked in your car with the engine running until you are positive that there is no threat. Consider not stopping at all and going straight away to the police or your embassy.

Much of the target hardening process is assisted by detailed information gathering and corporate headquarters should devote some of their staff to the business of maintaining 'running' files on all those countries to which they send executives. These files may be as simple as tourist literature: recommended 'no go' areas in various cities; hotels with built-in security and pertinent newspaper clippings. These should be regularly topped up with threat assessments from official sources or reputable commercial companies. They are an invaluable guide to the executive.

There are a few tips for the traveller which are worth considering. The first and obvious precaution if you are travelling to a high risk country is to make the visits irregular and ensure that they are as brief as the business allows. Do not advertise your journey; even limit the knowledge within the company. Do not use your own name for hotel reservations and do not reveal it until the last possible moment, i.e., when producing your passport at reception. In high risk areas good hotels are quite used to this and it will not in itself draw attention to you. By the same reasoning, do not use your company name for flight or hotel reservations. Always arrive at your destination with sufficient local currency to take you from the airport to the hotel. It is far better than advertising your presence by asking to be met, as this often leads to public address announcements and page boys with large indicator boards. Be inconspicuous, do not travel in expensive or eye-catching clothing; dress for the country or climate in which you are to land, even if this means being somewhat uncomfortable for a few hours at the departure point. Expensive suitcases and gold initialled briefcases are a giveaway. Go for chain store luggage. On departing the country, check your flight is on time, arrive early and go straight through immigration – in other words, wait in the area where the direct risk is the lowest.

Within every major city in the world there are areas where it is unwise to wander alone. Despite the temptations, and there may be many, resist the urge. Always have a member of the hotel staff hail a taxi; waiting outside or stepping into the 'one which happens to be there' is tempting providence. Avoid carrying your money in inside jacket or breast pockets or the back pockets of your trousers. These are the ones on which the pickpockets are trained and they are good! Carry cash and credit cards in side trouser pockets where they are best protected; remember it is not just cash you are looking after but identification which can tie you to the company or indications of personal wealth. You are vulnerable in a hotel so try to keep a low profile. Cafeterias are generally quicker and more anonymous than restaurants. Use the hotel safety deposit boxes and try to have the hotel staff note those occasions when people ask for you by name. On the phone to corporate headquarters develop the habit of talking in veiled speech or using analogies to pass on the details of your business.

What if the worst happens? What if you are kidnapped? Corporate reaction and the process of crisis management and contingency planning have been discussed in earlier chapters, but what of the individual? As in most situations, the victim has probably thought, 'It will never happen to me'. In that statement lies one of the reasons for the first reaction of capture. Blunt, stark shock. Freedom is gone! By being constantly prepared for the event the executive can spend regular amounts of time thinking about and understanding what corporate moves will take place. This is a great help in reducing initial shock, though it will not remove it completely. Kidnap is a brutal crime: it involves the emotional rape of both victim and dependent alike, to a degree out of proportion to all other crimes. Death by murder is far easier for a dependent to accept, especially if it is sudden.

The first consideration, after discovery that it is impossible to escape the ambush, is to recognise that to attempt to escape will probably be too dangerous. The kidnappers will be 'psyched up' and aggressive. They would not be in the business if they were not prepared to kill. You will initially be roughly treated in the haste to get away, but do not get indignant or aggressive yourself; the only reward will be a beating which you can do without at this stage. A ransom will be paid and you are going to survive – this thought must be uppermost in your mind. Accept that it is going to take a long time. Do not, at this or any other point, try to make a deal for yourself. The only result of this is the confusion of the crisis management team and the negotiator who will be working towards your release.

Take mental note of all you can which may help in any legal process afterwards but do this in an inconspicuous manner. If the criminals suspect that you will be able to identify them later, your chances of survival will be on the downward trend! Nonetheless this concentration will help to remove some of the numbing shock you will be feeling. Whilst still in this state of shock your mental resources are at their lowest and an experienced gang will know this. This is the time during which you can expect threats and rough treatment as the gang begins its interrogation of you. This will be in an effort to determine your wealth or the wealth of the company to assist them in setting a ransom figure. They are also alert for any remark you may make which may be of assistance to them in their negotiation.

You must now begin the process of 'setting your standards'. Decide upon a limit beyond which you will not go. Having decided this, stick to your guns. You are a valuable commodity to the gang only so long as you are alive and well. They will not risk overdoing the physical maltreatment, they do not wish to call in doctors. The emphasis is upon the 'reasonable' line of action. This could well earn you the respect of the gang but what is much, much more valuable is the fact that it is a vehicle by which you can cling to your self respect. In conjunction with this need for self respect, you should insist, as enthusiastically as you are able, on having the means by which to keep body and clothes clean. Resist at all costs the temptation to be physically or verbally violent. In fact go to the other extreme and retain good manners, politeness and dignity. Why die for an imagined principle if the only witnesses are criminals and thugs?

Your accommodation can vary from a cave to a reasonable room. Accept this, but remember the need for a cleanliness routine and try to develop a daily regime of washing, exercising and concentrated thinking. Do not argue with the quality of food. No matter how distasteful it may be, you need it and you may well get long periods without it; adopt a camel-like approach and store it. With a bit of discipline and some luck, you could emerge a mentally and physically fitter person. Think always to the future and devote mental energy on a regular basis towards planning. Keep a mental diary with hours as well as dates, and every day try to recall it from scratch. If this does not suit you then turn to chess or a hobby – anything which gives you the incentive to concentrate. Whatever you do, do not just vegetate. A good exercise is to review the actions that the corporate crisis management team will be taking which is another good reason why you should have a full understanding as to why it is such a slow and meticulous process. If you have a medical problem, then bring it to the attention of the gang. You may really need medication at some stage and, if it is a genuine provable ailment, it may well assist in speeding up your release.

In short, retain your dignity above all else, accept a potentially lengthy incarceration and maintain your mental and physical health. It will be seen that target hardening is a judicious mix of technical aids and an acute personal awareness and understanding which stretch from the learning process until well after, should an incident occur; the technical aids can be discarded but the personal awareness and will to survive are absolutely indispensible.

21 Executive Protection

Much of the business of executive protection was covered in Chapter 20 but here we reach into those aspects of corporate planning where the executive at risk may well have a hand in the structuring of the different phases of security; into the use of personal bodyguards; some important aspects of police and security forces liaison; and a discussion of kidnap and ransom policies as a precautionary measure.

The corporate headquarters employing travelling executives, and in effect placing them at risk on occasion, has indeed a duty to do its part in maintaining security. The executive, too, should understand what is involved and how the headquarters would perform, and thereby discharge its responsibilities, in the event of its own people being taken.

There is little mention here of technical aids to security except in the broadest possible sense. This is because training, education and continual awareness form the greater part of any security system and, apart from that, the plethora of equipment on the market today would require an almost encyclopaedic reference work in itself.

Chapter 18 explained risk management in detail, but here some thought will be given to those areas of direct importance to the executive in his office. In most cases the executives will form a highly valuable component part of corporate assets and yet their security is often taken for granted as soon as they step through the front door in the morning and touch their hats or nod to the glassy eyed security 'attendant'. It is this very atmosphere which has led to a rise in 'walk out' crime; this is particularly so in the USA. 'Walk out' is the technique whereby the executive is suddenly confronted in his office by the abductor and simply 'walked out' at the point of a gun to the waiting car. There are many simple ways of reducing this risk considerably; Chapter 20 mentioned the military principle of 'defence in depth' and corporate headquarters are usually well sited to apply this maxim.

Regardless of the style of the building, the outermost boundary owned by the corporation should be regarded as the outer perimeter of defence. Begin by restricting pedestrian access to one or two entrances if this is possible. At this entrance, initial staff pass scrutiny and bag searching can (and must) take place; visitors' credentials can initially be checked and to the would-be aggressor well organised security has its first deterrent impact on his criminal intentions. Metal detector loops and explosive sniffer systems can be set up at this stage within an 'air-lock' secured by ingress and egress doors remotely controlled so that the suspect can be held from advance or retreat if this becomes necessary.

Access by car or tradesman's van must be via one entrance with proper manned barrier control. All vehicle occupants must be identified. It is an old trick to gain access in a VIP vehicle and to be just waved through at the VIP's nod; how can the guard be certain that there is not a gun being poked in the known occupant's ribs? At this point all tradesmen and deliverymen are checked in and issued with time-expiring visitors' passes – they are then collected and escorted to and fro by a responsible member of the department with whom they have the appointment. This obviously applies to pedestrian visitors. Internal access control should be by means of personally accountable and registered access cards of which there are a multitude of efficient systems. If different systems are used for different levels of segregation or sensitive area access, then procedures to deal with the loss of such cards should already be in force, and must be rigidly controlled. When the headquarters layout is such that all executive management functionaries are sited in the same block then obviously a further sealed capsule can be constructed. If this is the case then give due thought to the effects of an explosive attack on so many targets within a small area!

When the headquarters of the executive is small, and it could be down to one office, then there are limitations to in-depth defence. In this event make the encapsulation as complete as is commercially viable. Closed circuit television (CCTV) with push-button, electronically-operated doors will suffice as a first line of defence but they should be backed up with a panic alarm system to the nearest support. Where possible, try to maintain an escape route through another door. Car parking presents a problem. It may be possible to 'leech' onto the nearby facilities of another company or park where someone else's security guard will (for a fee no doubt) keep an eye on your car. Best of all is a lock-up facility.

Precautions against stand-off attacks by machine gun, hand thrown grenades, rifle fire and anti-tank missiles are extremely unattractive but sadly necessary in some countries. Try, as an initial precaution, to have the executive offices sited at least three stories high to upset trajectories. It may be too expensive to contemplate armoured glass for the windows, but spall film can be used relatively cheaply with a two-fold effect: it will prevent or reduce the spalling effects from an explosion (splinters of glass which are thrown in all directions a high speed), but it can also drastically reduce visibility from the outside to confound the sniper. Wire mesh outside the windows is a definite help. Do not encourage the placement of objects in the office which will shatter in sympathy with an external explosion large glass-covered pictures, glass-fronted cabinets, etc., are al potentially the cause of severe secondary injuries. Car parking by the public can be a problem if the office is adjacent to a street. Little can be done about the potential car bomber under these circumstance except irregular but vigilant patrols by security guards. They mus have good liaison with the police or security forces where specialis assistance is at hand in the event of a suspect vehicle being detected

An increasing threat, which apart from the sheer menace can be laboriously time-consuming if proper preventive measures are no installed, is the explosive device which arrives through normal mai channels. Indeed much havoc has been created in some well-know companies just by the threat of these loathsome tactics. Loathsom because they are totally indiscriminate and invariably cause horrifyin gut-level and eye injuries. There is no real substitute for th installation of X-ray machines or one of the many different types o mail inspection systems. If these are installed and properly use then a stamp system to show that suspect packages have bee passed must be used. For the company or executive without suc facilities, awareness and intelligence are the defences he must fa back on. Firstly, resist the temptation to revert to human curiosit by bending or squeezing the package. There can be tell-tale signs o a package, as the 'plastiques' so favoured for these devices have tendency to weep after a period of time which can result in oil stains and sometimes powdery deposits as crystallisation occurs. smell of marzipan is indicative of one of the more commo explosives. Have a care however! If the device is properly constructe and the explosive contents have been professionally put togethe there will be few signs detectable by the human senses!

Do not be tempted to split open the seams or edges of a envelope or package to peer inside – this may be the very method initiation. Often a tiny hole can signify the withdrawal of a safet pin as the final arming device. The chances are that if the packag has survived your handling so far it can be taken to a safe place await the arrival of the experts. On no account place the package i water (as has often happened) as this will almost certainly cause any electrically dependent circuit to activate. Your awareness may be heightened by many different things: a spate of recent bombings by this method; a specific threat; hand-delivered mail which is not expected; unusually thick (6mm-plus) envelopes not anticipated and with no return address; or simply because of the nature of your work and environment.

Security begins at the desk whether it is at home or in the office. In the secure capsule the telephone does not appear to be a threat but the number of blunders made on this means of communication is incredible. Simple rules can avoid many slips. Begin by posting a reminder to yourself and your staff by putting a sticker on the phone which you will automatically see when calling or answering. Maintain control of the conversation especially on incoming calls – never volunteer information about locations, movements or identities. All such questions posed to staff should be referred to you. Confirmatory questions are usually the tactic of the terrorist: 'The office/house gave me this number and said he would be here, is that correct?' Careful education of staff in polite non-informative replies to such tactics is necessary. Answer a question with a question in order to elicit the name and contact number of the caller. For instance:

'Hello. Is that John Doe's number?'
'Good morning, sir. May I know who is calling?'

No information need be given away and the politeness is the perfect foil for the caller who pretends to get annoyed and aggressive. Staff can always fall back on the excuse that they are acting under corporate orders. By the same token do not put your name or the company name on an answerphone, simply state the telephone number. Do not even say '. . . the phone is temporarily unattended . . .', simply ask the caller to leave his contact details.

Bodyguarding is one of the most misunderstood occupations within the security arena. It is also an area which is full of muscle-bound 'machos' who may do well in a street brawl but who are virtually useless in the true professional sense of the business. The art of bodyguarding encompasses the martial arts as a last resort but first and foremost comes the ability to courteously and sensibly stop the charge from getting into a situation where these secondary skills are required. Against a well planned attack, a single bodyguard is useless and teams with good communications and planned back up are necessary. This is likely to be out of the reach financially, of the executive businessman. The hiring of a single escort, however, may often be possible and advisable. It is essential, when approaching a private company or agency, to be able to give a very complete picture of your business and personal lifestyle in order that men who will fit against your backdrop can be shortlisted for your selection. Whenever possible and if time permits you should insist on self-selection. You and the bodyguard are going to be very close over the working period and it is essential that you establish a good rapport from the beginning.

Your bodyguard is a highly skilled individual who should be able to instruct you intelligently and fully on all aspects of your security. He should display a working knowledge of the country you are travelling to and be able to forewarn you of any potential hazards at main airports and have a basic idea of the threats you may face. He must have armed and unarmed combat skills as well as a good knowledge of first aid. Searching buildings, cars and hotel rooms will be second nature to him as will offensive and defensive driving skills. Check his passport, international driving permits and innoculation records against the requirements of the country to which you intend to travel in his company. If you intend having him accompany you to important social or business functions, then tell him this and ensure that he has the facility to obtain the clothing necessities (a dinner jacket or dark suit, for instance), and check that he is aware of any etiquette requirements peculiar to the country. Once you are satisfied that he is fitted to your task, then accept him as an expert and heed his advice. You cannot, of course, put the full onus of the responsibility onto his shoulders; you must do your part. Discuss the problems openly with him and do not try to catch him out. In his field he is as expert as you are in yours and good bodyguards can generally pick and choose their employers far more easily than good executives can!

Do not use your bodyguard as a status symbol or 'show him off'. He is protecting you in part by his ability to remain inconspicuous and as such you should introduce him as a friend or colleague – a good man will, with a little briefing, be able to hold his own in any conversation without betraying his true role. If he suddenly snaps an order at you such as 'Get down!', do it! This man has accepted the responsibility of protecting your body with his own and he will not cry wolf. If you strike up a good personal relationship with your bodyguard, give him some indications of when you may like to have him in the future – if you are a good employer, he will do his best to make sure he is available to you.

Police and security forces liaison is a tricky subject in some countries. Where you are dealing with a stable, well ordered community but you know yourself to be at personal risk, it is usually the best thing to liaise directly with the nearest police station. Explain the threat and roughly what you expect to be doing. You will not be offered protection but you are going a long way towards ensuring that any serious concerns you have will be properly and promptly attended to. If you take this trouble at the beginning of the trip then you should also take it at the end, especially if you or one of your colleagues is to be a regular visitor. A contribution to the local police charity is usually viewed with favour but make sure that this is offered to a genuine organisation and cannot be mistaken as being a bribe! In less stable countries you are probably best advised to leave well alone. Instead alert your Embassy or consular staff as to your presence and the threat and then concentrate on personal target hardening.

An often discussed security aid is that of Kidnap and Ransom insurance (K & R). It is advised by many and despised by others. It would be as well to set the record straight and put it into perspective for the corporate headquarters and its travelling executives. Central and South America as well as Italy, Corsica and Sardinia all fall within the high risk areas where kidnap (both political and criminal) is a thriving business. The ransom 'going rate' in those countries, let alone the sums paid by those sufferers so unwise as to act without professional advice, are sufficiently high as to drastically affect corporate capital, to bankrupt small businesses and to destroy totally the lives of individual families. The possibility of financial loss causes us to accept completely insurance against injury, fire, theft, etc., so why not insure against another known risk which can be the precursor of severe financial hardship? Where is the immorality? The difference is that K & R insurance can only be effective if it is kept totally confidential. It is this confidentiality requirement which makes it 'non-declarable' and this has resulted in it becoming illegal in some countries because of the tax laws. This illegality in turn means that only a few brokers will handle it and it therefore becomes a very specialised and sensitive aspect of the insurance world.

These facts often face the potential client with an expensive 'take-it-or-leave-it' quotation. No broker would handle large fire or cargo prospects in this way and there is no reason why K & R should be treated as an exception. So where does this leave the corporate client who needs to cover business principals and executives against the kidnap threat? For many years Lloyd's of London have covered the risk. This is usually done using an indemnity policy whereby the client pays the actual ransom from within his own resources with reimbursement taking place after the Lloyd's assessors have conducted an examination of the incident to preclude the possibility of fraud (or collusion – as has happened!). The client will be dealing with a broker and not the underwriters and he will have to 'shop around' for the best deal. All K & R underwriters also retain the services of specialist consultants to provide advice to clients both in the precautionary measures to be taken against the kidnap threat and also to advise on the management of the kidnap negotiation if the client is unfortunate enough to become a victim. The object of K & R security consultancy from the firms retained by underwriters is in the first case to reduce the probability of a loss by the training and education of the clients since no amount of money can compensate the victim for such an ordeal: underwriters and clients have a common interest to this point.

The cloudy area occurs when it comes to the matter of *handling the loss*; this is primarily concerned with defining how much needs to be paid to obtain the release of the victim and the question is often asked, 'Is there a conflict of interests between the underwriter's agents and the insured victim?' An assurance against an affirmative answer to this question must be high on the shopping list of the potential client. Second must be the record of the broker in particular areas of the world. Although kidnaps and subsequent tactics are very similar in different threat areas, it is a fact that they are not exactly the *same*. Therefore a specialist in the geographic area is an obvious advantage. *In-house* surveyors and consultants are a further undeniable bonus; working exclusively for the broker, the doctrine of 'client first and foremost' is easy to maintain without being clouded by issues or accusations of 'underwriter loyalty'. An examination of the different threat areas of the world will produce a selection of salesmen and brokers in the K & R business but to take a non-typical example in a high risk area, consider KRI, based in Miami. The company has specialised in being an intermediary between clients and Lloyd's of London within the geographic area of South America (with the emphasis on the Latin countries). By judicious use of a 'wholesaler's' leverage, the company has achieved major economies in ratings for their clients; the whole enterprise is supported by the company's own in-house consultant service which operates both in the precautionary training and education role and in the area of negotiation advice should this become necessary.

In short, kidnap insurance and the inherent benefits, is a factor to be weighed alongside all the other rules, drills and preventive measures aimed at executive security which can be an important part of the overall safety screen.

22 Families and Dependants

One of the aspects of security which is continually on the mind of the executive, whether he is in his downtown office or in some far flung part of the world, is the safety of his family. Corporate headquarters will be aware of this factor and how such worries can reduce the efficiency of the executive. This will make them at least sympathetic to these concerns and some specific measures will almost certainly be taken to alleviate the problem. In the last analysis, however, the security of the family is the responsibility of the man himself.

There are more considerations here than merely the hardening of the executive target; quality of life becomes even more important and educational and domestic needs also have to be catered for sensibly. There is no doubt that if an executive is at risk from those who would kill or kidnap in order to bring pressure to bear or to extract a ransom of cash, then that executive's family is also at risk. The abduction of wives and children is, if anything, an even more effective means of extortion than the kidnap of a businessman. It is more emotive and the threats of rape, other molestation, beating and worse are far more fear-provoking if the victim is a woman or child.

What, then, can the businessman do which will enhance the safety of his dependents when he himself is absent from home? Once more the hardening measure becomes largely a matter of education with carefully explained rules and techniques. There are, however, some problems in that the last thing you want is to place undue stress upon the family by worrying them so much that their quality of life becomes unbearable. This can be completely counter-productive. The first lesson, therefore, is to conduct the education of the wife and family in a sane and serious manner without giving them cause to panic, and the approach is best calculated by the person who should know the family best – the husband.

Chapters 20 and 21 provide many of the rules and disciplines which are as applicable to the family as they are to the executive himself, namely, discretion, telephone discipline, the avoidance (where possible) of set routines, gates and garage security, and general common sense. There are, however, other aspects of life which need to be treated separately with regard to dependants. If some remarks are found to be offensive, the reader should remember that this is a broad brush subject and these remarks are born of experience.

The starting point as ever is the home. Top of the list is the fact that the family should understand fully the reasoning behind the security measures and have confidence in them and it is no bad thing to try to be anecdotal in the initial training of the family, especially when dealing with children. Secondly, it is essential that each member of the family and the domestic staff should know where to summon help by telephone or radio telephone at any given moment of the day or night. It is an obvious but nonetheless often overlooked fact that whoever the recipient of the 'assistance' call is, they should also fully understand the threat. Though this may seem to be common sense, and indeed it is, it is a fact that it may not be the police or corporate headquarters which is the first to receive the alarm, particularly if the family is living in an out of town area.

In keeping with the often expressed military principle of defence in depth, look first towards the protection of the home. There is a fine dividing line between what is acceptable and effective security and what measures will so restrict the normal course of life that they become intolerable. The executive and his family alone can decide where this line will be drawn but beware the paranoid tendency towards the 'Sangar' mentality. In itself it can be self-defeating, with total reliance on the system leading to a false sense of security and a blunting of the senses with the subsequent loss of awareness. Be sensible, let life go on as near to normal as possible but with the added precaution provided by a sound education into the whys and wherefores of simple rules.

The choice of house is important, but it is also appreciated that there will be limitations imposed which may be beyond the executives' control, such as finance, geographic area and the nature of domestic housing in a particular country. Generally it is possible to grade housing at safety levels in the following descending order:

Second floor and upwards flats in blocks with internal garaging and protected access by special key, communication or security guards (provided that 'escape routes' such as fire escapes exist).

A house within its own grounds where there is the freedom (and financial ability) to set up a phased defence system.

Others with varying degrees of suitability but where at least an
inner sanctum can be organised.

It is in and around the house which stands within its own ground
that there is the most scope for paying attention to security. The
appearance of the house is important for two reasons: the obviously
well-protected house has a deterrent effect but it can also draw
attention to the occupier. It may arouse the aspiring criminal's
curiosity and cause him to conduct a surveillance operation against a
target which he had hitherto not considered. Secondly, the 'sangar'
mentality, mentioned above, can be in part encouraged by
confinement within too limiting a space. Much depends upon the
size of the property and the distance between the perimeter and the
dwelling.

In an ideal world, a 2.5–3 metre wall of solid construction with a
sabre-tape top barrier (a refinement on barbed-wire which consists
of extremely sharp, flat, metal ribbon sections like razor blades)
which is alarmed would be perfect. Start with this as the 'ideal' and
scale the barrier downwards in direct proportion to the individual
needs, the laws of the land and the degree of visual interference
which the individual will tolerate. The guiding principle with gates is
that they should be at least as strong a defensive measure as the
perimeter itself. Top of the preventive scale for additions to a remotely
controlled gate is the fitting of a high quality CCTV system with a
low light level capability and a pan/tilt facility which allows cameras
to monitor given zones. This should be supported by the next best
thing, an efficient entry-phone system for remote identification of
visitors.

Perimeter lighting is a deterrent but so often it is wrongly used. If
there is an alarm system in operation to give you an early warning, it
makes sense that any lighting should cover the ground between the
point of warning and the next line of defence. As the next line of
defence is likely to be the outer wall of the actual residence and the
occupants do not want to be blinded by their own lights it stands to
reason that those lights should beam outwards from the house and
cover the ground immediately adjacent which should be clear of all
objects which could give cover to an approaching aggressor – in
military terms, the creation of a 'fire zone'. If dogs are to be used, it
should be remembered that only a well trained animal is of use.
There are far too many 'tricks of the trade' in the criminal's arsenal
to make even the best dog more than a deterrent part of the

concept. Again, beware the false sense of security given by the beasts.

With regard to the doors in the immediate line of defence (house outer wall), be guided by common sense; ask yourself the question: 'Do I have to open this door to see who is on the outside?' This is a seemingly obvious point but one that is frequently neglected in otherwise excellent security systems. Peepholes, illumination, deadbolt systems and flush fitting edges are essentials to door security. If the entry-phone or other system fitted to the door makes it necessary for you to have to stand in close proximity to the door in order to answer the call then consider the fitting of bullet-proof barriers to preclude the possibility of being sprayed with machine gun fire. Reduce the number of doors which are in frequent use to the absolute minimum remembering the possibility that an escape route may still be needed as a part of the overall security plan.

Windows, whichever floor they are situated on, are a hazard. Remove all natural and unnatural means of climbing to upper storey windows and if in doubt treat them to the same conditioning as ground floor openings which must be externally barred if they are to provide any security whatsoever. Beware the surveillance threat and consider heavy drapes and the installation of one-way visibility spall film as described in Chapter 21. The greater the number of outer wall potential weaknesses, the more attention must be paid to the hardening of the inner sanctum. These inner rules apply equally to flats as well as to detached hourses.

The inner sanctum can be in any convenient room in the house which lends itself to the situation but it must fit within certain parameters:

It must be rapidly accessible to all members of the family at any time of the day or night.

It must have external communication to the point of immediate support, preferably radio telephone.

It must contain the list of blood groups, emergency telephone numbers, radio call-signs, etc. referred to in Chapter 21.

It must house an up-to-date medical kit.

Food and water, especially to cater for the needs of infant children, if necessary, must be stored within.

Stow in this room any weapons which are normally kept in the house.

Before any firearm is used study the dangers of discharging it
within a confined space. It should be a last resort only.

Games or toys to divert the attentions of the younger children.

Observation ports (peepholes in doors/windows) are very helpful
in assisting the occupants of the room in providing instant
intelligence to the police whilst they are en route to assist.

This is your last bastion and therefore the doors should be as secure
as possible as must the window; seriously consider armouring here
even if it has not been carried out elsewhere in the house.

The education and training of domestic staff is fraught with
problems especially if the staff have been with the family for a long
time. Remember, no matter how long they may have been around,
they are not members of the family! You simply cannot afford to
invest them with the same degree of trust as you would bestow upon
your wife or any other intimate family member, for instance. Apply
the 'need to know' principle rigidly. Obey simple rules when
selecting staff. Background information in the form of references is
essential and **must be checked**. Copies of all identity documents
should be kept within a safe inside the inner sanctum or lodged with
your bank and, what is more, the staff should know that you have
taken this precautionary measure. If your corporate headquarters
does not have the facility to conduct a 'vetting' operation of your
staff on your behalf, contact the police and explain the situation and
invariably they will be willing to help in the case of a serious
request. Get to know your staff and as much as you can about their
personal circumstances; learn their habits and expressions as all
these factors can be an invaluable early warning to you if they are
under duress to provide information about you and your family.
Generally speaking staff are very vulnerable and historically they
have been the initial targets of many a kidnap and assassination
operation.

Although in a marriage the presence of children is very rewarding,
in a threat situation it is extremely problematic. Children love to
boast, they enjoy mystique and drama; secrets to children are
almost meant to be shared and this is as dangerous as it is inevitable.
Accept this and do not be tempted to display all the security
measures to them – content yourself with a lucid and non-dramatic
explanation of the facts relating to the awareness you are asking
them to adopt and teach them some simple rules, all of which can be

covered in analogy form under a different reason, for example child molestation or even the threat of a simple robbery.

Always insist on knowledge of the child's whereabouts and explain why you need to have this information. If you do this, you must reciprocate and always let your offspring have a telephone number where **you can be contacted** if you have to leave them alone in the house. This establishes the rules of fair play. In this topsy-turvey world of criminal child abuse it is now commonplace for children to be educated at school and home alike as to the dangers of conversing with strangers and accepting lifts. Amplify by warning your children and explain that they may be approached in the quest for information about their parents' occupation, movements and habits. Instil in them the importance of telling you about attempts to question them and encourage them to remember as much as they can about the physical appearances, speech characteristics and the like of their questioners. Remember children's propensity for exaggeration and vivid imagination and pay attention to this if what they have to say leads you into contacting the police.

Make the children aware of the tactic whereby they can be asked to convey a false message, often a dramatic one, in order to get a member of staff or family to open an otherwise well-controlled door or gate. Give them simple instructions in the art of telephone answering and especially ensure that they never give away those occasions when they may be alone in the house. Teach them the rudiments of travel awareness. If possible they should not mount or dismount the school bus at the same point every day unless protected by the company of other children or parents who may be meeting or escorting them. The message is: if in doubt do not dismount – travel another couple of stops and contact your parents.

With teenage children it is difficult to get them to 'come clean' about their various friends and acquaintances; they may harbour doubts about your ideas on suitability. This is natural, but at that age the child should be capable of understanding the reasons for your concern and will hopefully co-operate with you. It is an unfortunate reflection of the 1980s but drugs and sexual promiscuity are prevalent and certainly in the case of drugs they take the child into the direct clutches of organised crime. This obviously dramatically increases the risk of kidnap of wealthy youngsters. Little can be done about this except repetition of the normal parental exhortations to resist the temptations of drug abuse and to be aware of the signs and symptoms in order to be forewarned about the two-fold dangers.

A question is often raised about whether a child should resist an attempted abduction. This is a particularly sensitive area and it must be a parental decision, but some factors should be considered. It is certain that an attack on a youngster or a woman, if the general public is aware of it, is far more likely to bring assistance than an attack on a man. It is really a matter of whether the would-be kidnapper is armed or not. If he is not then it would be logical advice to kick, scream, scratch and bite generally attacking the obvious area of the assailant's eyes, testicles and insteps. It is exceedingly difficult to maintain a hold on a fit young child who is determined to escape. Italian records throw up many cases where youngsters have foiled the kidnappers on public streets by adopting the 'kick and holler' tactics.

Whilst on the subject of children, what about the very young infant? Such offspring need the open air as much as adults and it would be foolhardy to walk them in the parks and public gardens in high risk areas unless bodyguards are hired. Sadly, if the house has no garden or such area then there is no recourse but to revert to the hospitality of friends. There is nothing wrong in this but again remember that it must not be done on a predictable regular basis.

There will be occasions when the family, with or without the husband, will be returning to a house which has been left in the care of staff and this is the time when the true value of one more well-established but oft-forgotten ploy will be seen. Teach the staff the dangers of your position during these moments and arrange with them some form of coded signal to alert you to the presence of danger in the house. These signals should take the form of an action which a member of staff can carry out without placing himself/herself in danger such as the removal of an obvious ornament from the window, the drawing (or not drawing) of a particular set of curtains or perhaps the switching on or off of a particular light. Ally this to a simple veiled speech system on the telephone where certain apparently innocuous phrases can confirm the presence of danger when you make the follow up call. 'I look forward to your return', or something similar, can mean, 'Don't come back!'

There is another area of family education which sadly may be necessary. That is the preparation for the release of a husband or child who has been a kidnap victim and may have been kept in unpleasant surroundings for a considerable time. Although this is generally a time for uninhibited happiness, on the majority of such occasions there can be complications. Most victims make an effort to get on with the gang in order to make their own conditions as comfortable as possible, but this is no guarantee that the gang will be telling the truth when talking to the victim. There will be occasions when the victim has heard terrible stories about the family's callousness in refusing to pay the ransom and in haggling over apparently small figures. If the victim does not understand the negotiating principles and the reasons for them, there is a very good chance that he/she will begin to nurture a hatred of the family. Do not worry, this is a temporary state of affairs. The important thing is to arrange for a proper reception. A doctor should certainly be on hand, even though there may have been no intimation at all as to the victim being ill. Although huge relief is the normally expressed and apparent emotion, there will be a need for supervision for a few days at least. The victim may not be able to sleep and will certainly be nervous, so tranquilisers may be needed. He/she may have been on a very deprived diet for some time and care will have to be taken over the amount and rate of eating for a while. It is always a good idea if a short holiday can be arranged in the company of family members only. There is a need to get away from the questions of the police and the newshounds; the victim will almost certainly be short tempered with these people for a few days as conversation may have been severely curtailed for long periods.

There have been extreme cases of emotion, to do with the well known Stockholm Syndrome, in which victims have become particularly close to their captors. This probably started out as an attempt to ease their own comfort but developed into something more powerful. Education of the family by experts is the answer. They will then better understand the problem of the Stockholm Syndrome, and why negotiations can be such a time-consuming affair. This puts the time in capture into perspective. Next, for the family to try to imagine themselves in the same surroundings as the victim will help to develop an understanding of the emotional turmoil which is present on release.

In summary, the security of the family basically follows the same common sense lines as the strategy for target hardening the individual, except that it is an area where positive attention has to be paid to the stresses potentially imposed upon the wives and children by too frightening a briefing. It calls for a deeper knowledge of the family and staff under more personal circumstances than other areas of security and a requirement for a great deal of tact and trust within the immediate family. The most difficult area to accept, calls for an active but hidden mistrust of staff who may have been in the household for years. The stories are legion of people who have been given away for various motives by 'trusted servants and retainers'. 'But she was almost a member of the family!' has been a common cry. Don't let it happen to you.

Index

Index